Remembering G.K. Moopanar

About the Author

Prof. Ganapathi Palanithurai, Coordinator in Rajiv Gandhi Chair, Department of Political Science and Development Administration, in Gandhigram Rural University, Tamil Nadu. He is also associated with Centre Planning Commission, State Planning Commission of Tamil Nadu, Population Foundation of India, Ford Foundation, UNICEF, Rajiv Gandhi Foundation, CAPART, Ministry of Rural Areas and Employment and DANIDA (Danish-Indo Development Agency) in specific areas of activities in connection with empowerment of people.

Prof. Palanithurai has to his credit fifty-eight books and one hundred and twenty seven articles on three major areas, namely, legislative behaviour, ethnicity and Panchayati Raj System. He was recipient of Fellowship from Sastri Indo-Canadian Institute, New Delhi and World Academy of Art and Science, USA. He is the Chairman of the Tamil Nadu Council for Sustainable Livelihoods. He was a visiting fellow in the McGill University, Canada in 1989. He is a member of the expert committee constituted by the Government of Tamil Nadu to monitor the training programme for local body leaders.

Remembering G.K. Moopanar

G. Palanithurai

CONCEPT PUBLISHING COMPANY PVT. LTD.,
NEW DELHI-110 059

ISBN-13: 978-81-8069-678-7

First Published 2010

Published and Printed by

Concept
Since 1974

Concept Publishing Company Pvt. Ltd.
Regd. Office:
A/15-16, Commercial Block, Mohan Garden
New Delhi-110059 (India)
Phones : 25351460, 25351794, *Fax* : 091-11-25357109
Email : publishing@conceptpub.com
Website: www.conceptpub.com

Editorial Office:
H-13, Bali Nagar, New Delhi-110 015, India.

Cataloging in Publication Data--*Courtesy:* D.K. Agencies (P) Ltd. <docinfo@dkagencies.com>

Palanithurai, G. (Ganapathy), 1953-
Remembering G.K. Moopanar / G. Palanithurai.
p. cm.
G.K. Moopanar, 1931-2001, politician from Tamil Nadu, India.
Includes index.
ISBN 13: 9788180696787

1. Mūppaṉār, Ji. Kē., 1931-2002. 2. Politicians--India--Tamil Nadu--Biography. 3. Tamil Nadu (India)--Politics and government--20th century. I. Title.

DDC 954.05092 22

TO

THE DIVINE MOTHER

Preface

On the day of G.K. Moopanar's demise I was in New Delhi and I was not able to attend his funeral, but, on the subsequent day, I attended the rituals for the disposal of the ashes from the place of cremation. When I came to the spot where G.K. Moopanar had been cremated, his interactions with me came to me as glimpses. It was always a joy to hold conversation with G.K. Moopanar. I was so fortunate to have conversed with him on many critical issues of politics, and society on many occasions. I enjoyed the conversation on all occasions. I have met many political party leaders in my life. On all the occasions, baring a few, the majority of the political leaders used to speak and make others listen. But G.K. Moopanar was an exception. He was a good listener. He was extraordinarily patient to listen to the views of others. Even while listening he used to intervene softly and gently to make others feel comfortable. One could find a tinge of sarcasm also at times.

I was witnessing the rituals performed by his son G.K. Vasan. I felt that it was not just a personal loss to a family but a loss to the country, to his political party and to democracy. It was a sorrowful day for me. On that day, I was thinking about the void created by G.K. Moopanar's death in Tamil Nadu politics. He was a man of peace and compromise. He did not adopt any unethical means to reach power. He was not power hungry. He was not after possession. He was not aggressive. He was totally against the politics of violence and vengeance which we witness today. Hence it was really a big gap created by his demise. On that day I decided to register some of the important conversations which I had had with him and some of the questions he had raised and which I had answered. The discussions between me and him were on some of the important critical issues and ills in Indian polity and society. His role in Indian and Tamil Nadu politics was important and critical and has to be studied in depth since it was remarkable. He belonged to a different category of leaders who were known for their honesty, integrity, sobriety and simplicity. He was from a political school which was known for its decent democratic political culture. His approach, style and behaviour were totally different from the ordinary.

The younger generations of today in Tamil Nadu are witnessing the politics of hatred, conflict, anger, meanness, mistrust—politics of defaming one another in the lowest order between the ruling party and the opposition parties. Now this culture has gone to the other States and upto New Delhi also. Normally democracy helps society to reach maturity. Democracy provides opportunity to society to evolve towards higher levels of activities. But, to handle democracy, society needs understanding and skill. Political leaders should take up the responsibility to prepare society collectively to handle democracy. Unfortunately, in many countries, political leaders have gone astray to catch a power instead of creating a culture favourable to democracy. But, at present, in Tamil Nadu, the trend is regressive. Instead of moving forward it moves backward. Democracy tends to solve problems. It has got tremendous potential to solve any kind of problem within its framework, provided society is able to handle it. Theoretically, democracy has such potential. The potential is being used very effectively in the west and western countries are fine tuning the same to suit the contextual requirements. In India, the same democracy creates problems and conflicts. It is always a question why in one set of societies, democracy works well and delivers good and why in another set of societies democracy does not work well. For many, democracy means elections alone. Democracy has been conceptualized in India in this way only. People do not know even how an election has to be faced. Winning elections is the only target for many political parties, leaders and people. How it is won? is yet another issue. Thus all political activities are oriented towards elections and nothing else. So the totality of political culture is not understood and the totality of democracy is not perceived. Democracy has a wider meaning and a broader perspectives. Democracy is a culture and a way of life. Respecting each other, appreciating each other, conducting oneself in a dignified manner and treating others in a dignified way are the values that count in a democracy. It culminates in the total culture of a society. In a democracy, the leaders are the role models. The leaders have to show the way. For a vibrant democracy, dignified and cultured leaders are imperative. The leaders should be sensitive to the values of democracy. In this context, one can imagine what kind of strained relationship is maintained between the ruling parties and the opposition parties and legislatures in India at present. Attacking each other in vituperative language and denigrating each other ruthlessly ruin the image of the leaders and democratic culture. Mutual mistrust, antagonism, hatred and defaming each other in politics make the people believe that leaders are dishonest and they are not respectable. Thus democracy has been portrayed in a bad light. Our political leaders have been shown in a bad light. When they denigrate each other and defame each other, the common people think ill of them. Moreover, in the past sixty years of our experience, we are not in a position to say that our representative democracy has evolved and attained maturity. In fact, it is receding instead of progressing. It is only through a responsible and mature leadership that democracy can be saved and nurtured.

At the dawn of Independence, our economy was weak, our administrative set up was weak, our scientific and technological capability were not as they are today. Yet our leaders' views were valued in the world. Our leaders never aligned with any country and took a strong position. Our leaders established creditability among the people. But now the conditions have changed. Even the tallest leaders are shown in a bad light.

All these happenings are the creation of our leaders. People, before they understand the values of democracy have been oriented in elections, not in democracy. It is the sorry state of affairs in Indian democracy. Why is our democracy always deficit? One ready-made answer is that Indian democracy has been imposed on our people. They did not demand it. They never fought for it. They did not struggle for it. They fought for freedom. It was our elites who decided on the nature of democracy to be adopted for India. Western democracies are "evolved" democracies. People were involved in the struggle to establish representative democracy and equally people fought for their franchise. But in our country both were thrust on us. Adult franchise and representative democracy were granted without any demand from the people. But to run this democracy people need awareness and understanding about the systems. People have to be oriented and socialized for democracy. This process needs a band of committed leaders who have unshakable faith in the people and democracy. Many countries in the world committed themselves to representative democracy after their liberation from the colonial yoke but, within a short span of time, they drifted away from democracy. In this respect one has to appreciate our founding fathers, especially Pandit Jawaharlal Nehru. The biggest contribution of Jawaharlal Nehru is the establishment of representative democracy in India. Till date, parliamentary democracy survives and it will survive. It is because of the leadership that we had at the dawn of Independence. In this context, I value the democratic leadership of G.K. Moopanar. He was an ardent supporter of democracy. G.K. Moopanar was a great democratic leader, who had unshakable faith in the people and democracy. He was sober, sensitive, people-centric, and humane. He was always powerful without being in power. He demonstrated that even without holding positions one can serve society and the party. He belonged to a rare breed of leadership.

But now, unfortunately, our people are oriented in the electoral process very intensively and not in the larger democratic culture. Our elections and the processes have brought intense conflict among the political parties and the leaders. In this context, a leader with immense faith in democracy and people is an asset to democracy. G.K. Moopanar always represented the common man, even though he hailed from an affluent family. An agriculturist's background with riches will produce only a feudal leader. But, contrary to such expectations, this background produced an extraordinary leader in democracy. That was G.K. Moopanar!

In a short span of time I keenly watched him and closely moved with him and I found rare qualities in him and that is why I want to write a short sketch about him from my own perception. Though I moved with him closely only very briefly he left an indelible mark on my memory and that is why I want to bring out a monograph on G.K. Moopanar. Secondly, I want to produce a good analytical biography about him later as he was like K. Kamaraj, and other tall leaders. First, I saw him in my native village when I was a student in a Panchayat Union School in the 1960s. But I moved close to him after only he founded the Tamil Maanila Congress. Thiru P.V. Rajendran, former M.P. and MLA, was instrumental in making me move close to G.K. Moopanar. In fact he introduced me to him as a Professor working in a Gandhian Institution. Subsequently, G.K. Moopanar gave me a few assignments. The assignments were purely academic analysis of political trends I carried them out. I did it for him. I found some party men were suspicious about my association with G.K. Moopanar as if I was working for seeking a ticket to contest in the elections. Later, they realized that my association was purely intellectual. Here I register my thanks to Mr. P.V. Rajendran for having introduced me to G.K. Moopanar.

G. Palanithurai

Contents

Contents

1

Introduction

In India, ordinary citizens do not have the needed awareness and understanding about governance and administration which are mystified and complicated. Hence, for everything people look for help from politicians. Politicians act as a bridge between the government and the people. In India 72 per cent of the people live in rural areas. Of them around 60 per cent rely on agriculture for their livelihood. Indian villages are governed by the dominant class and caste through a feudal system. People go by the community norms in social relationships and the Constitution has no role in the rural areas. For the success and survival of representative democracy enlightened and vigilant citizens are the basic requirement.

India is a populous country deeply committed to democracy and for the past sixty years Indian democracy has been serving in different forms despite the presence of extreme variations and differences in terms of social, economic and cultural conditions of different segments of the Indian society. India is always a paradox and a world laboratory to generate theories and ideas on society, governance, politics and administration. No other society has such a variety of differences and variations. Theoretically speaking, the conditions which exist in India are not conducive to the functioning of democracy. Democracy will function better in a less conflicting situation. In India, we witness extreme social conflicts as a result of the uneven development taking place in the Indian society. Development-driven conflict works against the smooth functioning of democracy. Politics intensifies the divisions in the society, which is divided on social bases and conditions, for the maximization of benefits. In general, democracy is expected to solve the problems in the society by which it enables the society to attain maturity. But, contrary to expectations, Indian democracy creates problems and conflicts. Despite all weaknesses and shortcomings India survives as a democracy. It is a paradox which is called the 'Indian paradox'.

In my opinion as a student of politics, democracy provides only opportunities but these opportunities are to be used for the benefit of the society. It depends on the people and the leaders, and more particularly on the leaders, because the society is being guided only by the leaders and it is being socialized only by the leaders. The role of the leader is crucial in a democracy. Leaders are recognized as individuals with distinct qualities to lead the masses. They are visionaries. Their perception, behaviour, attitude, vision and performance at every level will shape the society, governance, administration and development. Unfortunately, now the leaders are becoming rulers. In India, it requires a lot of energy to orient the people and take them to politics for political action. Hence, our leaders are becoming rulers and thereby they rule the masses. People have to be led for which people have to be prepared, oriented and socialized.

Leaders are not born but groomed. They are being shaped. There have been leadership schools in the world right from the days of Socrates down to this day. In many western universities leadership schools are functioning. Leadership courses are being offered and these schools are drawing students from all over the world. Then, there are specialized institutions organizing periodical training programmes for the leaders. In the same way even political parties have such programmes. Only in India, our leaders are not undergoing any training in any school. Our leaders' perception is also different. The junior leaders are oriented and shaped by the senior leaders. Even in leadership, there are different kinds. We have business leaders, party leaders, leaders of administration and group leaders. There is one category which is totally distinct. They are people's leaders or mass leaders. The mass leaders are able to attract the people by their distinct

qualities. These leaders need not necessarily be the leaders in power. Infact, they never seek power. For them, their personality, commitment, sincerity, openness, simplicity, love for humanity are their power. Without wielding power, they are able to mobilize the masses.

Leaders like Mahatma Gandhi, Nelson Mandela, Martin Luther King Jr. belong to this category. These leaders prepared the masses for transformation through a struggle. They were not in the framework of a system. They performed all their activities outside the system to orient the people and the system. There were leaders who orient the people within the system. The leaders in democracy have to manage the institutions and the people. Ethical values are given a back seat as these institutions are to be managed effectively by keeping the people vibrant as voters. It is a moot question how democracy is shaped and in turn how democracy shapes the society.

To answer the above questions one has to understand the status and position of people in a society. In democracies, one will find Her Excellency President of India, Honorable Prime Minister, Honorable Ministers, Honorable Chief Ministers, Honorable Members of Parliament, Honorable Members of Legislative Assemblies and respected officials but the common people are the most disrespected and humiliated. They are treated as beneficiaries, dole receivers, petitioners and voters but not as citizens. Even the people do not perceive themselves as citizens with self respect. They never have the feeling that they are shaping the government. People who assume power by getting votes from the people are not sensitive that their position is due to the people. They keep their eyes on votes and never look beyond them.

While giving benefits to the people, the representatives who are in power presume pressure that the benefits are given to the individuals by the representatives as if the people are destitutes and the representatives are the saviours, as if charity government schemes are being distributed to the beneficiaries. People are not in a position to claim their entitlements as rights. The whole exercise disempowers the poor. Respecting the people is a culture. It is the basic indicator of a democratic culture. People in India tend to surrender their rights to the government along with their responsibilities with the attitude that everything will be taken care of by the government. But when the government fails to address issues, the people start giving petitions to the government as petitioners. It is argued that India is a socially hierarchical society with a feudal mindset and so one cannot expect that the poor and the underprivileged will be treated honourably. Only through struggle equality is achieved in the world. The moment they take the petitioner's stance, they lose their self-respect.

In such a context democracy needs a new type of leadership to empower the poor. Societies like India have different social groups and those who are on the side of power will always be assertive and aggressive. They are the real managers of democracy. While managing democracy and representative institutions, people have to be oriented in such a way that both people and democracy have to evolve and one will be able to see the complementarity of both. But, in reality, despite all development, the impact of democracy has been dwindling. In this context, leaders with sensibility and sensitivity towards the people and people-centric democracy assume significance.

There are certain individuals, in all different circumstances, who play a crucial role silently in resolving crises, problems, may be in the party or in governance or in administration without making a noise and without power and authority. In this category is found G.K. Moopanar who played a significant role in Tamil Nadu and Indian politics.

In this small monograph I endeavour to highlight his views and observations on many critical issues of our society, governance and administration. It is presented in the form of conversations between G.K. Moopanar and myself. These dialogues were held on a number of occasions. They have been presented here to present G.K. Moopanar as the uncommon leader of the common people!

2

A Short Biography of G.K. Moopanar

G. Karupaiah Moopanar known as G.K. Moopanar and affectionately called Ayya, was born on 19th August, 1931 in a rich landlord's family in Thanjavur District. Kabisthalam is his native village. Govindasamy Moopanar and Saraswathi Ammal were his parents. Later his father shifted his residence from Kabisthalam to Sundaraperumal Kovil. His father Govindasamy Moopanar extended all possible assistance to freedom fighters who participated in the freedom struggle, since he was although an ardent supporter of the Indian National Congress. His family was known for charity in those historic days, as it is mentioned in history.

G.K. Moopanar had his early education in his own native village and higher schooling in Papanasam. He could not continue his education beyond high school as he had to share the family responsibilities with his father. Having the background of a rich landlord's family, he inherited the key features and characteristics of a rich farmer's family. They are: hospitality, charity, listening to classical music, loving traditional arts and so on. G.K. Moopanar's family is known for its joint family system. Till date it is a joint family.

G.K. Moopanar had three sisters and three brothers. His marriage to Kasthuri Ammal was solemnized traditionally in his native Sundaraperumal Kovil on 1st June, 1949. He had a son named Govindavasan (Now G.K. Vasan) and a daughter named Usharani. Both graduated from city colleges. His family is not only known for charity but also known for piety. Much of the lands of the family had been donated to different temples long back, even before the Land Ceiling Act was enacted. His

G.K. Moopanar and his brothers

family had created a charitable trust for Lord Sri Venkateshwara. By the munificence of his family many temples had been renovated. All national leaders who visited Thanjavur during the formative years of Independence visited the native village of G.K. Moopanar as his family played a key role in deciding the socio-political activities in this region. From the first general elections onwards G.K. Moopanar actively participated in the activities of the Indian National Congress. In fact G.K. Moopanar met K. Kamaraj in his house in the year 1951. G.K. Moopanar was introduced to Pandit Jawaharlal Nehru in front of his house in Sundaraperumal Kovil by K. Kamaraj, when Nehru visited Thanjavur.

When he was 24 he lost his father. His increased workload in public activities, coupled with higher responsibilities in the family after the demise of his father, enhanced his capacity

G.K. Moopanar Garlanding Nehru

also. Fortunately, his brother Rengasamy Moopanar came to the aid of G.K. Moopanar which enabled him to concentrate on public activities. Till his demise and even after that all the family responsibilities were and are with Rengasamy Moopanar. Though he worked for the Congress candidates in the first general elections, formally he joined the National Congress only in the year 1956. In the same year he was elected member of the Pradesh Congress Committee at the age of 25. His committed party activities without having any formal position earned him the post of District Congress President of Thanjavur District in the year 1963. He was elected to the position. From 1963 to 1976, he held the post of District Congress President and it was considered a glorious period for the Indian National Congress as he kept the party units vibrant and active.

G.K. Moopanar met Indira Gandhi in the year 1965 when she visited Thanjavur District as Minister for Information and Communication. During her visit to Thanjavur District, she made a personal visit to G.K. Moopanar's house. During his tenure, he engaged the party not only in party activities, but

G.K. Moopanar Garlanding Rajiv Gandhi

also in development activities. A series of programmes were organized. He emerged as a tall leader in the District Congress and he acted as a leader of the District Congress family. The Indian National Congress faced a split in the year 1969, and G.K. Moopanar remained with K. Kamaraj till the merger of the Congress (O) with the Congress (I) in the year 1976. All through G.K. Moopanar remained a loyal servant of the Indian National Congress and was equally loyal to K. Kamaraj. He performed the rituals for the ashes of K. Kamaraj in

G.K.Moopanar with his Family Members

G.K.Moopanar in a ritual

Thiruvaiyaru after the demise of K. Kamaraj and he was seen in the eyes of the party men not as a loyal party worker but as a son of K. Kamaraj. He performed the rituals as any son would perform them for his father.

Even when K. Kamaraj was alive, he had determined to integrate the Congress (O) with the Congress (I) for which he took steps and shape. But, unfortunately he could not see the merger comes true. After the demise of K. Kamaraj, G.K. Moopanar took steps to fulfil the desire of his leader K. Kamaraj. After the merger of the Congress (O) with the Congress (I), the Indian National Congress became vibrant and active and hence G.K. Moopanar was nominated Pesident of the Pradesh Congress Committee. During this period, he tried his best to mobilize membership for the party by his yatra to various places. During the Emergency he was the President of the Tamil Nadu Pradesh Congress Committee. It was almost like the Chief Minister's Post. Yet he never misused his office. After the Emergency, the 1977 general elections to Parliament turned negative to the Indian National Congress and it was defeated. As he was with K. Kamaraj, G.K. Moopanar stood

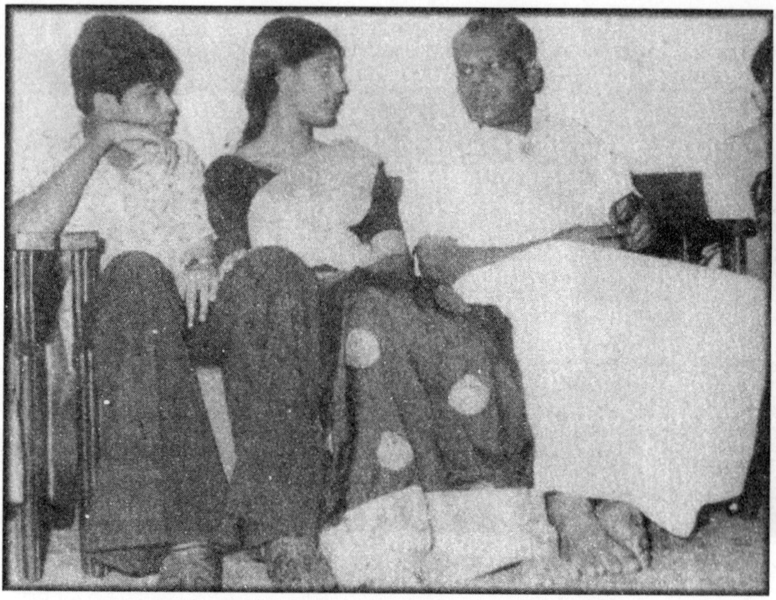

G.K. Moopanar with his son and daughter

like a rock with Indira Gandhi during the turbulent days. After Indira Gandhi became the Prime Minister in 1980 G.K. Moopanar was made a General Secretary of the party.

He continued in the post till 1988. He served with Sanjay Gandhi and Rajiv Gandhi as General Secretary. He was the longest General Secretary in the party. As he always evinced balance and equipoise in his approach and temperament, he managed to solve many problems in the party. He was a leader with extraordinary commonsense and human relationship qualities and hence he emerged as an accepted leader of many of the groups in the party. But, in the year 1988, Rajiv Gandhi nominated G.K. Moopanar the President of Tamil Nadu Pradesh Congress Committee with a view to strengthening the Tamil Nadu Congress Party.

During his tenure as President of the Tamil Nadu Pradesh Congress Committee, G.K. Moopanar organized an All India National Congress Committee conference in Chennai in the year 1988. After he became the President, the members of the

G.K. Moopanar's Parents

Indian National Congress hoped that this party would capture power in Tamil Nadu as people were fed up with both the Dravidian parties. Moreover, they felt that they had a leader with a national stature, and a leader having accommodating tendencies. The Indian National Congress decided to fight the election in Tamil Nadu alone with a view to capturing power and establishing Congress rule. People called it the "Kamarajar Rule". In the 1989 general elections to the Tamil Nadu Legislative Assembly, Tamil Nadu Congress Party contested alone without forming any alliance with any major political party. It contested in 209 constituencies. But it secured only twenty six seats. But it improved its vote bank under the leadership of G.K. Moopanar. He became the Legislative Party Leader of the Indian National Congress. He held the position from 1989 to 1991. From 1991 to 1995, he was not in any position and yet he was active in party activities during that period. In 1995, again he became a member of the Rajya Sabha. In the year 1996, the Indian National Congress, under the leadership of P.V. Narasimha Rao, took a decision to face the general elections in Tamil Nadu with an electoral understanding with the All India Anna Dravida Munnetra Kazhagam (AIADMK),

G.K. Moopanar with his Father

against the wishes of the Tamil Nadu Congress Party. Against this background, G.K. Moopanar formed the Tamil Maanila Congress (TMC). The Tamil Maanila Congress forged an alliance with the DMK and emerged victorious. In the subsequent elections, it went without any alliance with the DMK or the AIADMK. In the general elections to Legislative Assembly of Tamil Nadu, it aligned with the AIADMK. In the last phase, G.K. Moopanar had a feeling that the TMC had to be integrated with the Indian National Congress. Even in the electoral understanding with the AIADMK, he made it

Condoling the Demise of G.K. Moopanar

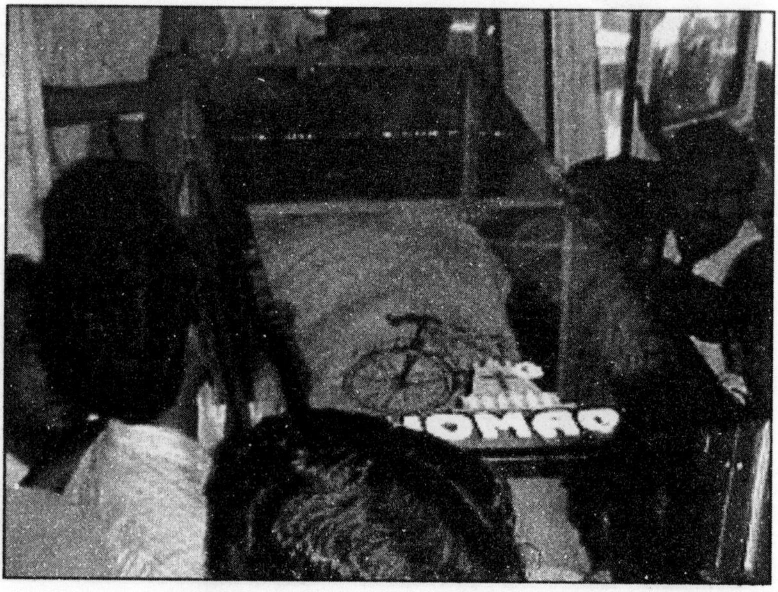

Condoling the Demise of G.K. Moopanar

Condoling the Demise of G.K. Moopanar

inclusive of the Indian National Congress. As K. Kamaraj did when he was in the last phase of his life, G.K. Moopanar also prepared the TMC for a merger with Indian National Congress.

Unfortunately, he breathed his last on 31st August, 2001, before he could see merger of the TMC with the Indian National Congress. He was a rare brand of politician. He was a multifaceted personality. He always went beyond politics. He nurtured good relations with politicians of all political parties. He had good relationship with many intellectuals and he was fond of intellectual discourse. He was a lover of music, art and culture. He led a very simple life which made him draw the attention of all.

3

A True Congressman

On the day G.K. Moopanar came to Madurai to release the biography of the late Kakkan, a former Minister who served under K. Kamaraj in Tamil Nadu, I was asked to meet G.K. Moopanar in the Tamil Nadu Hotel. I reached Madurai around three o'clock in the afternoon. The moment I reached the hotel, I was taken to his room by Mr. Sakthi Vadivel. He was with a few leaders in his room. The whole hotel was jam-packed as the party workers had thronged there. Within a few minutes all were moved out. He asked me about my panchayat activities and I explained to him about the capacity building exercise which was going on in the campus. Women and Dalit panchayat leaders were being trained continuously. (I will explain later why he raised this question).

Then he made a statement to me just as we present statements to students in the examination to comment upon. His statement was: "In our party, namely, the Tamil Maanila Congress, a few leaders are putting up an argument that Mamta Banerjee came out from the Congress and formed a regional political party and she is going to be the Chief Minister in West Bengal. We have also formed the Tamil Maanila Congress with G.K. Moopanar as our leader. But the way in which he leads does not show us a way to reach power. Look at the DMK chief. Despite ideological differences he moved over to the BJP and captured power. His party men are happy. But our leader by citing ideological reasons, refuses to go along with the DMK to the BJP. As a result we have lost a chance to share power along with the DMK. These are the observations of our party men and women. Kindly explain, if it is correct".

Leader with his Political Guru

I asked a few questions. Is capturing power in Tamil Nadu the only objective of your quitting the Congress? Are you willing to give up the basic principles of secularism for the sake of power? Mamta Banerjee would go to any extent to unseat the Communists from power. Would you adopt the same strategy adopted by Mamta Banerjee? Can you engage in politics by pursuing a course of conflict? You have come out from the Congress Party. It is always natural that when a

breakaway group forms a new party after coming out from the parent body, the leaders of the breakaway group attack the parent body and criticize the leader of the parent body to justify their action. But, in your case, you have been asking your party men not to criticize the Congress Party and its leaders. You have your own pattern and culture. Against this background how will you adopt the stand of Mamta Banerjee? As long as you heading the party your party would not take the stand of Mamta. In the past three decades, Indian politics has become very aggressive and conflict oriented. Mamta has

G.K. Moopanar with Rajiv Gandhi

taken a position to be in the existing culture and course. But you are dissuading your cadres to avoid the existing political culture of violence. Against this background, how do you justify taking Mamta Banerjee's position in Tamil Nadu politics? These were the questions raised by me. To all the questions he answered in one line.

He replied that he was and he is and he will be a Congressman. "I cannot think of any party other than the Congress, the Indian National Congress. Further, though I formed the Tamil Maanila Congress, I cannot have a principle which is contradictory to that of the Indian National Congress. Nowhere are we different from the Indian National Congress. While functioning we maintain autonomy but in ideology there cannot be any major deviation from the Indian National Congress Party. I cannot abjure secularism for a few seats and to satisfy a few Congressmen in my party. The DMK may have that flexibility and it might have switched over to the BJP. I

G.K. Moopanar listening to Smt. Indira Gandhi

cannot give answers to the people as the DMK gives. I will not commit such a blunder in my life even if I become unpopular. I am in the party as leader to earn self-respect for the party men and women and not as a middleman to earn positions for a few and make them happy. I know pretty well that ideology does not attract people at present as positions and power do. But I cannot move on this path as the other parties do." These were the statements made by him.

I observed: "By sticking to your ideological ground you have succeeded, by which your secular credentials have gone up. As long as you proclaim that you are a Congressman, you cannot move away from the ethos of the Indian National Congress." I reminded him of the speech delivered by C. Subramaniam and writer Jeyakanthan in the conference organised by the Tamil Maanila Congress to chalk out its vision, mission and ideology. In that meeting at Aathur (a place near

G.K. Moopanar with K. Kamaraj in a meeting

Listening to K. Kamaraj in a meeting

Listening to K. Kamaraj in a meeting

Chennai), C. Subramaniam underlined that the Tamil Maanila Congress was born not out of an ideological crisis in the Indian National Congress and that under the leadership of G.K. Moopanar many Congress workers came out from the Congress Party because of the decision taken by the national leader to align with a political party which was criticized as totally corrupt at that point of time. Beyond that there was no ideological difference. Hence, the Tamil Maanila Congress must stick to the basic ideological principles of the Indian National Congress. In the same way writer Jeyakanthan said that it was only circumstances which made G.K. Moopanar and the Congress workers leave the Indian National Congress and form the new party and, in the same way a new set of circumstances would emerge by which it could be integrated with the Indian National Congress. In this context, the Tamil Maanila Congress has no option but to stick to the ideology of the Indian National Congress. I also spoke in the same meeting with a different background. I said that the Congress had a sound ideology but it was not contextualized. Ideology has to be contextualized to accommodate changes. The Congress does not incorporate the regional aspirations of the people. Moreover, it has to change its style of functioning. The traditional vote banks were moving away from the Congress about which nothing was being done. In this context the Tamil Maanila Congress should have an ideology which is totally contextualized. Moreover, the regional aspirations are to be accommodated. It should be a regional party with a national outlook. It should be people centric and it should be inclusive.

G.K. Moopanar posed another question. "Some journalists and well wishers have stated that I have failed miserably or I have committed a tactical mistake by aligning with the DMK after the formation of the Tamil Maanila Congress to face the elections. The trend was very positive towards the TMC when it was formed. If it had contested alone as TMC in the elections, the TMC would have won the elections. It would have formed the government in Tamil Nadu. Is thus a correct assessment?".

I replied "The mood of the people was such. They were tired of the DMK and the AIADMK. But where was the organizational backup for the TMC? The TMC was born. It was a mass party all right. But there was no organizational backup. Of course people expected that the TMC should go it alone in the elections. But how could TMC reach power? You have not done any mistake. The DMK had the organizational structure which helped the TMC to emerge victorious. By seeing the mood of the people everyone felt that the Tamil Maanila Congress could have contested alone. However weak organizationally the TMC was, people would have gone to the booth to vote for changing the fate of Tamil Nadu. The mood of the people made everyone think like this. Had the TMC taken the risk at that point of time, the party would have been in power now and it would have emerged as a regional political party with a national outlook. Unfortunately, it was not the case and G.K. Moopanar had declared that the DMK was a

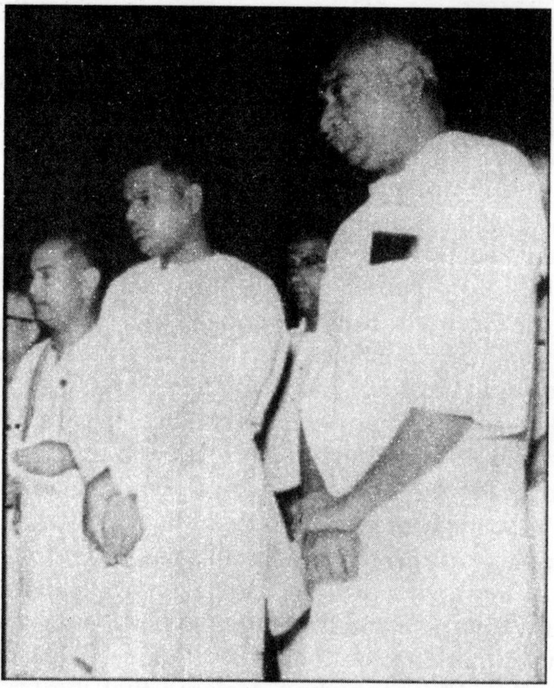

G.K. Moopanar with K. Kamaraj in a meeting

G.K. Moopanar with Smt. Indira Gandhi

clean party. But it was considered a grave mistake committed by G.K. Moopanar. Moreover, after some time the crowd usually coming to Satyamoorthy Bhavan (TMC office) has started dwindling. People who had moved over to the TMC got disillusioned as party workers were not engaged politically with a sense of commitment and vision. There was no organizational structure to absorb and engage them for its political activities. Within a short span of time after the TMC's victory, it could have created such structures. But there was no such step. It was a total failure. The weakness in the Indian National Congress continued in the TMC also." When I gave this reply he said, "Yes, I was totally responsible".

When I got this reply I felt bad and wondered if I had committed a mistake by projecting the negative points of the TMC. But one thing I admired in him was that he boldly accepted the failure and took responsibility. It is a remarkable quality.

I came to the old argument. The Tamil Maanila Congress was not born merely to capture power. It had to capture power

G.K. Moopanar dining with party workers

G.K. Moopanar in a party meet dining hall

through a means which is acceptable to the ethos of the Indian National Congress. I said, "As long as you proclaim yourself a Congressman and you refuse to move away from the Indian National Congress, you cannot compare yourself with Mamta Banerjee." When I made this observation he said that he wanted to be a Congressman with a tradition nurtured by K. Kamaraj. It is a very rare quality among today's leaders. I have seen many Congressmen who have moved away from the Congress ideology and tradition but are still in the Congress. G.K. Moopanar, by his thought and action was a true Congressman. I realized this only on that day.

4

An Unforgettable Event

One day, I went to his house along with the veteran Communist Leader Thiru Nallakkannu and another comrade from the Communist Party of India (Marxist), Mr. G. Ramakrishnan, to arrange for the releasing of my book on Panchayati Raj. I had written a book which is a manual for Panchayati Raj leaders. I requested G.K. Moopanar to release the book and he agreed to do so. But he asked me "Who will receive the book"? I said leaders from the Communist Party of India and the Communist Party of India (Marxist) would. Immediately he himself contacted the Communist leaders over the phone and fixed the date for the book's release. He made it a very simple function. I suggested that the function should be held in his house itself. It should be a symbolic one. There would not be any speech making.

When it was finalized, an unexpected event happened in Tamil Nadu politics. Dr. Kalignar was arrested and he was taken to prison. I was wondering whether my book release would be held as per schedule or not. When Dr. Kalignar was arrested actually, the Tamil Maanila Congress was with the AIADMK alliance. The AIADMK was in power. Actually I reached Chennai on the day of the book release. First, I went to the office of the Communist Party of India (Marxist) and met G. Ramakrishnan (Executive Committee Member of the Party). G. Ramakrishnan and I went to the office of the Communist Party of India. We met Mr. Nallakkannu and he in fact asked me a question about the arrest of Dr. Kalignar. I said that it was not fair on the part of the political parties to

G.K. Moopanar with the author releasing a book

keep silent on this issue. "If anything untoward and unexpected happened to M. Karunanidhi, history will not forgive you". It was the statement made by me. He in fact asked me to make the statement in front of G.K. Moopanar. We reached G.K. Moopanar's house around 10, o'clock. The moment we reached

G.K. Moopanar honouring Dr. G. Palanithurai with Shawl

G.K. Moopanar releasing the book, received by Shri Nallakannu

his house, he, in fact, raised this issue. Whatever I had stated in front of the Communist leaders was repeated in front of him also. In his usual way he stared at me. Then he asked the two Communist leaders about the issue. All of them discussed that issue for some time. I came out of the room as they wanted to discuss other political issues and their stand. After some time I went inside where all of them were discussing the same problem.

All of them had agreed to issue a press release in which the leaders had decided to request the Government of Tamil Nadu to release Dr. M. Karunanidhi. When this was prepared in his office, one prominent leader from the Tamil Maanila Congress requested G.K. Moopanar to take a careful decision as the TMC was in the AIADMK front. Unmindful of the observation, he asked Peter Alphonse to draft a press release and got the signature of the representatives from the two Communists parties and affixed his signature too. In front of his office there was a crowd. It was a team of press persons. The press was invited to cover the book release. But they were restless in the morning itself. More than the book's release, the press was waiting for some statements from these leaders on the arrest of Dr. M. Karunanidhi. The book release function was secondary to them. G.K. Moopanar assessed the mood of the press. Finally, G.K. Moopanar came out and issued the press note. After ten minutes' gap, the book was released. It was received by Mr. Nallakkannu and the other leaders. While releasing the book he said that the panchayat system has to be strengthened for which lot of activities have to be done by the government, civil society, and the political parties. He further said that the panchayat leaders must read the book and run the administration and administer development. Once the programme was over, I went inside his room and he asked me about the press release I said "You have done the correct thing". He smiled. Without following any formality, he did everything for my book release and despite his indifferent health on that day he released the book written by me which I will never forget in my life. The same book was revised, updated and published subsequently. But we have lost G.K. Moopanar. My friends asked me in whose presence the revised book was to be released. I said it had to be released only by G.K. Vasan. In the same way as his father did, Vasan released the book and the leader of the left political parties received the book. It was also a memorable occasion.

After a long time when I met him in Satyamoorthy Bhavan, G.K. Moopanar casually asked me. "What is the reason for asking the left leaders to receive your book?" I replied that in the whole of the country, it is only the left parties that are sincerely committed to the Panchayati Raj System. The left political parties sincerely believe in the Panchayati Raj System. They respect the people and that too the poor. They strongly strive to empower the poor and for them Panchayati Raj is a powerful instrument. In my opinion the left leaders have identified themselves with poor and common men and women. Hence, I thought that the left leaders were the right persons to receive the book. "You are correct," Mr. Moopanar replied. He continued, "Have you heard about the Panchayati Raj System nurtured by our leader K. Kamaraj?" I said, "yes". I further told him that the Tamil Maanila Congress has to work for such a vibrant Panchayati Raj System in Tamil Nadu. He agreed that it was our duty.

5

Concern for the Dalits

In Indian politics one can hear the noise raised by many for the upliftment of the Dalits and the other marginalized groups. But their conditions remain the same and there is no improvement substantially on the part of the Dalits. I went to Moopanar's place to meet him casually. On a particular day, surprisingly, G.K. Moopanar asked me a question: "I was told by many of the party men and women that I have invited trouble to the party by keeping Dr. Krishnaswamy and Mr. Thol. Thirumavalavan with our party by which non Dalit vote banks have moved out of the party. The two leaders are leading caste based parties and hence they should not have been included in the alliance to face the election. Further, some of my party men lamented that the DMK and the AIADMK have kept these two leaders away for long. The reason is that once these parties (DPI and Puthia Tamilagam) are included some of the castes will move away from the parties which formed electoral alliance or at least they will not vote for the party which is in alliance with the Dalit parties. What is your opinion?" To the above question I replied: "You have branded yourself an ardent Congressman. Congressmen have to work for the upliftment of the Dalits. The Dalits were the traditional vote banks of the Congress Party but the Dalits have moved over to other parties now. Why have the Dalits moved over to the other political parties? They felt that the Indian National Congress would not look after the issues of the Dalits. In Tamil Nadu, the Dravidian political parties have absorbed them. But now they have started moving away from them also. Now they are coming closer to the Tamil Maanila Congress. Moreover,

G.K. Moopanar with Dr. Krishnasamy and Thol. Thirumavalavan

you had no option but to go with the Dalit parties. Further, we have to consider the lamentation of B.R. Ambedkar that the problems of untouchability would be solved only when the communities which were responsible for this kind of oppression realize the plight of the untouchables. They have to work for the upliftment of the Dalits. The Dalits now want not only reservation but also recognition. You are recognizing them and there is nothing wrong in it. If you align with any other caste based parties, you have to be criticized. One has to understand the pitiable position of the Dalits. Primarily they are living in sub-human living conditions. When they are living in sub-human conditions naturally one cannot expect that they will respond always positively. At the same time, policy-makers and decision-makers are not sensitive to the problems of the Dalits. Their feelings, emotions and pains are not properly understood. Against this background what will they do? All the time they make noise. In order to bring them into the mainstream, it is necessary that the Dalit parties have to be accommodated in the electoral alliance formed by the national and regional political parties. Further, their issues have to be taken up for policy advocacy by the mainstream political

G.K. Moopanar with Thol. Thirumavalan

parties. Such a course will assuage the political tempo of the society, especially in tackling the issues of the Dalits."

He further asked, "What are all the activities to be initiated for Dalits by the Tamil Maanila Congress?" I said, "First you have to create a cell for Dalits; second, a vibrant leader should be chosen for the activities in the cell; third, the Dalit issues have to be focused upon along with other issues; wherever the Dalits are affected, the cell has to organize meetings and involve the party leaders in addressing the issues of the Dalits; an annual convention has to be convened and they have to be allowed to voice their feelings and emotions, and, finally on each issue a policy note is to be prepared for the party leader". G.K. Moopanar asked yet another question; "To what extent has the Dravidian movement helped the Dalits? Where have they fulfilled the task and where have they failed?"

I replied, "The intentions of the Dravidian movement cannot be questioned. But, while taking up activities for Dalit

G.K. Moopanar with Party Members

emancipation, they were not as effective in action as they were in speech. Upto the middle class and lower middle class, the Dravidian parties have reached but they could not reach the unreached. Tamil society takes resource allocation as a dividing line." G.K. Moopanar stopped me by saying "K. Kamaraj appointed Thiru Kakkan as a Home Minister". "It is true, but it was very rare", I said. I continued further, "The Congress, by its action and appearance is a feudal party. It will not provide space for the middle class. This was the impression given to the people". This perception motivated the middle class to move towards with the Dravidian political parties. The Congress in Tamil Nadu has a perception about the OBC issue but the Indian National Congress does not have the needed perception on the OBC issue. The Tamil Maanila Congress has its own perspective in the line of K. Kamaraj. K. Kamaraj had a clear perception of the reservation issue but he could not influence the Indian National Congress on the issues of the OBC.

He intervened, "How are we to sensitize the party men on this issue? They understand the need for reservation but it is very difficult to sensitize the party men on this issue."

I said, "It is a problem not only for the Tamil Maanila Congress but also for all the political parties. Otherwise, the problem of untouchability would have been solved long back."

G.K. Moopanar asked further, "To what extent will the New Panchayati Raj System help to solve the problems of the Dalits?" So I explained the scope of this new dispensation. At the same time I indicated the problems involved in it. At this point he asked, "To what extent are our communities mature enough to understand this issue and allow the Dalits to empower themselves?" I said that it all depended on how effectively our government and political parties work vigorously on this issue. Finally, he said, "In a representative democracy, addressing these vital issues is difficult as the system depends on the votes." After a few months he made an announcement that whenever he goes out of Chennai for party work, he will dine in the house of any party worker, preferably a family of Dalits.

6

On Reservation of Seats for Women

I went to Moopanar's office on (Asoka Road) one day to make a courtesy call. On the previous day, I had participated in a women leaders' meet and made a presentation and it had appeared in *The Hindu* which I had not yet seen. The moment I entered his room he asked me about the programme. I told him that the meeting was intended to exert pressure on the Central Government to bring in early legislation to provide reservation of seats for women in State Legislatures and the National Parliament. "Will it happen soon?" he asked. I said, "Not today, it will take its own time and for that we have to struggle". He told me that, for this, first women have to be sensitized and oriented to demand legitimately what is due to them. I requested him to speak out on this issue. He informed me that Mrs. Jayanthi Natarajan had been entrusted with this task.

He again posed a question: "Can you tell me from your experience whether women's participation in governance has made any difference?" I have explained accounts from Western countries as a backdrop. He immediately interrupted and asked me to focus on India and more specifically on Tamil Nadu.

I said, "Yes, no doubt, women representatives have enormous barriers and problems and yet a large number of leaders have emerged as independent achievers. Women leaders have their own perspective, understanding and vision. I have met a large number of such women leaders." In fact I have written a number of monographs on the achievements of the elected women representatives from Tamil Nadu titled

"Path Finders". Later these were published by Concept Publishing Company as a book.

He interrupted, "Is it the story of all women panchayat leaders?" I got the point and replied, "Not all the leaders are free from the clutches of patriarchy and community control. It is true that many women leaders are asked to remain in their houses and all the office duties are attended to by their husbands, brothers, sons, fathers-in-law and so on." He turned our discussion to another area: "Palanithurai, explain to me why two Yadavs, both Lallu Prasad Yadav and Mulayam Singh

Yadav, are opposing women's reservation. Are they really anti-women?"

I said, "It is not so. What they want is internal reservation within reservation for women. OBC and SC/ST have to be given seats separately. This is their contention. Unless you give such reservation, this will benefit only the upper caste and forward community women, not the backward caste ones. This is their argument."

He asked me another question, "Is it really correct?" I told him that logically it is correct, but practically in the absence of such a break up in census data, implementation will be difficult. Moreover, it is perceived that both leaders know this background and yet they are making such a demand in order to stop this process. But one cannot deny their logic or repudiate it.

"The OBC issue is a very complicated issue in Indian polity and society. It is always dividing the society," observed G.K. Moopanar. I replied, "The Indian National Congress generally failed to understand the issues of the OBC and their implications." Hence the Congress Party did not address the issues of the aspirations of the various segments of the society. Till date the Indian National Congress has not learnt lessons from its own experience. In Indian polity the OBC issue is a serious issue. It was K. Kamaraj who quickly grasped the issue and acted firmly. It is a model to all other states in India. Unfortunately nobody followed it. What he did in Tamil Nadu was not advertised. If the Indian National Congress had followed the model of K. Kamaraj in this regard, the exodus of the backward class cadre could have been averted. In the same way the Dalit issues were not properly looked into and, as a result, the Dalits moved away from the Indian National Congress. When I made this statement, he asked, "Why are you so emotional?" I said, "I hail from a humble and rural family and rose to this level because of K. Kamaraj. It was he who gave reservation of seats for BC people in educational institutions. Till date I feel indebted to K. Kamaraj."

Subsequently he asked me another question: "What is the logic of demanding 33 per cent of seats?" I said, "It is nothing

G.K. Moopanar receiving a reception

but the model of reservation followed in the Local Bodies. There is one strong logic in the number. If the number goes down, there won't be any use at all. Above 10 per cent is the critical number. Hence in the Indian context one-third is considered to be a critical number."

Finally, I put a question to G.K. Moopanar: "Don't you want reservation of seats for women in the State Legislatures and the National Parliament?" He replied, "Palanithurai, I want reservation of seats for women, but which "women"? You have to understand. It is not a woman from the traditional political base or from the urban base. She should be a woman from the village. Such kind of women have to go the National Parliament and State Legislatures. Honest, sincere, committed women have to go and they should be from the rural areas. If there is such a policy I will welcome it." With this I concluded my interaction with him and left his room.

7

On the New Panchayati Raj

G.K. Moopanar was an ardent supporter of Panchayati Raj and a believer in grassroots democracy. But he believed in the trustee system. People's leaders should have commitment towards the work of serving the people. The elected grassroots leaders have to treat the office as an office of service, not as an office for profit. He was much worried about the corruption seen in the development programmes. In fact, on many occasions he told me that the panchayat system nurtured by K. Kamaraj was the ideal one. He further told me that K. Kamaraj strongly believed that in all development works people should be made stakeholders and the leaders at the grassroots should be made their trustees. He further elaborated that K. Kamaraj, when he was a Chief Minister, kept the Local Body fortfolio with him. In his opinion, the Local Body was the best instrument to orient the people in democracy and make them claim their entitlements. He deeply felt that the framework had been diluted to serve the party people through the State Government machinery without the interference of the people. Thus the Panchayati Raj Act of 1958 enacted by K. Kamaraj was weakened and diluted to the maximum. A State which was once a model for the implementation of Panchayati Raj was transformed into a model for weakening the Panchayati Raj System!

After the introduction of the 73rd and the 74th Amendments to the Constitution of India, Tamil Nadu, under the AIADMK, was reluctant to enact the conformity legislation. Even after the enactment, there was procrastination in conducting elections. In order to exert pressure on the State Government, I organized several programmes through Gandhigram Rural Institute. Finally, I approached Justice V.R. Krishna Aiyar. He told me that nobody could go to court on the ground that the Tamil Nadu Government had not conducted elections to the Local Bodies as there was no mention in the Constitution about the non-conduct of elections to the Local Bodies in a state where Local Bodies were not in position.

I met many leaders of the political parties and convinced them. I spoke to Maalan, a writer, who was with Sun TV as its news editor. In the same way I spoke to many leaders. But the DMK manifesto and the manifestoes of other political parties profusely stated that they were committed to conduct the elections to the Local Bodies. In the same way the TMC also included it. In the general election, the DMK and the TMC emerged victorious. After the elections I went to G.K. Moopanar and requested him to take steps to conduct the elections as promised. Moreover I explained to him about the legality involved in it. Wherever the Panchayati Raj System was in vogue, the panchayat elections had to be conducted within six months if panchayats were dissolved.

In the case of Tamil Nadu, there was no Panchayati Raj System when the 73rd Amendment was introduced. Hence, if the DMK decided not to conduct the elections, legally no action could be taken. This was the position. When I explained this position to G.K. Moopanar, he told me that the Chief Minister would not go back on his assurance. Even then we should exert pressure on the Government through our own members in the Legislative Assembly. This was the reply given by him. The panchayat elections were conducted and the Local Bodies were positioned. How to orient the elected Local Body leaders was a major question.

In Gandhigram Rural University, a chair was created in the name of Rajiv Gandhi. It was created with the objective of creating a movement from below for strengthening the Local Bodies. This chair was financially supported by the Rajiv Gandhi Foundation. In the whole country it was the first chair created for Panchayats. (Now there are ten chairs funded by the HRD Ministry). It functioned for some time and, after some time, the BJP came to power. No support came from New Delhi. People advised me to change the name of the chair. Against this background I went to G.K. Moopanar and explained to him about the condition of the chair and its financial crisis. He asked me to meet C. Subramaniam as he was the chairman of the Congress Charitable Trust. I went to C. Subramaniam's house and I explained the situation to him. He told me that the Congress Charitable Trust had to support all the Panchayati Raj activities of the Rajiv Gandhi Chair. He encouraged me to continue the work. He further asked me to inform G.K. Moopanar that he had agreed to help. Finally, I got money from the Trust. After getting money from the trust, periodically I informed and reported to C. Subramaniam about the Panchayati Raj activities undertaken by the Chair. G.K. Moopanar told me one day that all good works are always supported by many. He asked me to continue the work. Wherever I met him he used to ask me about the progress of devolution and Panchayati Raj activities. I used to explain the position and about our activities. He used to ask me what should be done to strengthen the panchayats. Normally I used to carry with me a written statement. I handed over the paper to him. The next day I saw his statement in the press. Whatever points I had given were there in the statement. He was always keen about our Panchayati Raj activities. He was one among the few who supported me in my Panchayati Raj activities. In the same way the Left political parties asked my opinion. I used to prepare notes for them also on Panchayati Raj. Many times I told Moopanar that I was meeting the leaders of the Left parties on Panchayati Raj matters. He always encouraged me. In this way he made me a Panchayati Raj man.

There was an yet another occasion when he asked me a question: "What made you move close to the Left Front leaders?" I replied, "In my opinion, in India the Left political parties are the only parties who believe in the people, respect the people and work with the people. All the other political parties developed pity/sympathy for the poor people. But the Left parties work for them and work with them. Moreover, it is the Left political parties which respect the people that too the poor. The Left political parties are with the poor. They are for the decentralisation of power. They are pro-poor parties. Against this background I think that the Left political parties are the appropriate parties to be contacted for political interaction."

He further asked a question, "Is it true that the Left political parties have used Local Government as an instrument to deepen their hold on society?" I replied, "Yes. I was told that it helped them to some extent. What prevented the Congress Party from using the same for their expansion? Even Rajiv Gandhi quoted this model." Finally, he said that the strengthening of the Local Bodies would take a long time. It needed consistent work on the part of the political parties, civil society organizations and opinion makers. I replied that Rajiv Gandhi stated that to take proper shape the panchayat will need minimum of twenty-five years. It has its own process. We have to act and wait up to that period.

8

A Democratic Leader, Pure and Simple

Being a true follower of K. Kamaraj, Moopanar led a simple life. It was reflected in every action of his. He mostly wanted to be with the people. At every level he saw that the life style should not be changed. While writing an article on K. Kamaraj, he expected that every politician should follow a simple life. The existing disparities between the rich and the poor are vast and people feel that they are alienated from the Government. Moreover the present democracy and the Government will not work for the poor people. People who become politicians are prospering but they do not solve the problems of the poor. The common people are not treated as citizens. They are considered dole receivers and beneficiaries. This trend cannot continue any more as people will be totally disillusioned over the system of governance and administration. Governance is mystified and administration is complicated. When governance and administration are not understood what will the common people do? Naturally they will go to the politicians and they will act as brokers.

G.K. Moopanar was serious about keeping his life style very simple. He did not want to lead a luxurious life. Even in food habits too, he preferred only simple food. He would eat with party men and friends. His office and other rooms were kept as simple as possible. His life style reflected the life of a farmer. His house and office would give the look of a farmer's house.

K. Kamaraj insisted that our politicians had to present a simple appearance and they should lead a simple life. By doing so they could make the people have faith in the politicians and

the system. Once I had the privilege of visiting G.K. Moopanar's house in Sundaraperumal Kovil where I met his brother Thiru G.K. Rengasamy Moopanar. After a brief chat, he asked me to join him for lunch. I accepted the invitation.

Around one o'clock he asked me to go with him to the dining hall where I found there was no dining table at all. [In Tanjore, the custom is to spread a mat on the floor to sit on. In front of the mat, leaves (Banana leaves) are spread]. A simple delicious vegetarian meal was served. It was very very

G.K. Moopanar with Dr. M. Karunanidhi and Actor Sivaji Ganesan

ordinary. All vegetables were drawn from the local place. Fruits were drawn from their own lands. Such a simple life style was reflected in the Chennai house also. At every level I saw the simple life style. I wondered whether this was indeed the life style that was advocated by K. Kamaraj.

Moopanar was a highly democratic leader. Democracy means maturity, understanding, respecting others and their

G.K. Moopanar with EVK Sampath

views. That is why John Stuart Mill wrote that democracy is suited to only a few societies which are highly matured. For the success of a democratic regime the society should have the requisite maturity. The leaders should orient the people in the democratic process. It is a very difficult process. In many developing countries, people are mobilized only on the emotional plane. Against this background the leaders have to orient the people in democracy. Democracy is negating violence. All issues can be resolved through the democratic process and that too through dialogue.

G.K. Moopanar was a great leader in this respect. He could have wangled many positions if he had so desired. He was not after position. But he wanted to have a high value profile of democracy. Respecting the views of others, avoiding confrontations, allowing others to express their views,

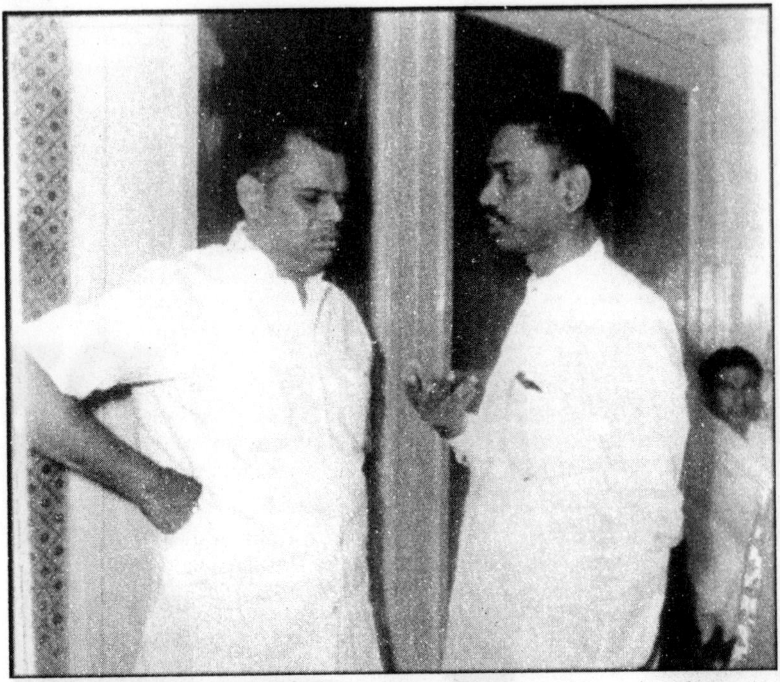

G.K. Moopanar with P. Nedumaran

considering the views of others in decision-making were the fine qualities of G.K. Moopanar.

On one occasion, many of the Tamil Maanila Congress (TMC) leaders, especially the second line leaders, argued that the TMC had to act independently and take up the people's cause and struggle to mobilize the masses by which the party could emerge as a major political power. There was yet another group which strongly argued that this was not the time to do it as the party had been perceived as an ally of the ruling party, the DMK. He was in a dilemma. On this question I expressed my view to G.K. Moopanar when I was asked to do so by him.

I told him, "You were a crowd puller during the election time. Your views were heard and respected. But now you do not form part of the ruling party but, at the same time, your party is considered an ally of the ruling party, yet, your party has been recognized as an opposition party. Now you have to play a role by which you have to support the ruling party and by which officials have to obey you. At the same time you have to mobilize the people to get their grievances redressed by your intervention. You have to express your views on issues fairly. When need arises you have to criticize the ruling party also. Then only your party will be consolidated. People have to be mobilized. Once they are mobilized, they can be consolidated. In the whole process your party will be engaged and strengthened. You have to orient the youth also as they show interest in violent politics. The DMK and the AIADMK have developed a new political culture. It is a culture of mutual animosity, mutual degradation, mutual insult and ultimately they have cultivated a politics of violence for survival. Against this background, you have to show a model which is totally committed to democracy and development. Your focus should be on democracy and development. All the activities of the TMC should be for development politics."

After a few days, he started on a tour. First he visited Tanjore area to meet people and interact with them. It is a general tendency in Tamil Nadu that the opposition party has to oppose the ruling party forcefully and criticize the ruling party. People are oriented to enjoy this culture. In this political culture, he wanted to follow a different path. He made observations sometimes critical, but they were subtle, certainly at the higher level. While meeting the people, he listened to them and promised them to redress the grievances by taking them to the appropriate destination. He attracted the crowd. Unfortunately he could not continue the project further as his health did not permit it. It is unfortunate that the second level leaders could not chalk out a programme to effectively mobilize the people through this method. G.K. Moopanar wanted to be different in his approach. He proved to be a leader with difference in terms of democracy and development. He was a popular leader, pure and simple.

9

Treating Everyone with Utmost Respect

One day I went to his house to meet him. He was not well on that day. When I reached his house I was told that he was with a couple of visitors. I was told that it was an unscheduled meeting. I was sitting in the drawing room. After half an hour, I saw two great Gandhians, Jegannathan and Krishnammal Jegannathan, coming out and they were accompanied by G.K. Moopanar. Despite his illness, he accompanied the couple up to their car. He opened the door of the car and asked Jegannathanji to get into the car. I was carefully observing his gestures and interactions with the couple.

Once they got into the car he requested Krishnammal to take care of Jegannathan as our society needed Jegannathan for a long time. When he returned after sending off Jegannathan I accompanied him to his room. It was my usual routine that whenever I met G.K. Moopanar, I handed over one "blessings packet" of Shri Aurobindo Ashram to him. Even on his birthday, I never send any message or greetings. He will not be in his house on his birth day. He used to disappear. But I used to pray for him in my meditation room. On this day I gave a "blessings packet" to him. In all humility, he received it and touched the "blessings packet" to his eyes. He knew how to respect the sentiments of other people.

He asked me to look at a photograph on the wall of his room. It was a photograph taken during the visit of Pandit Nehru to Sri Aurobindo Ashram. It was one of the rare moments and a rare photograph. The photograph carried the images of the Divine Mother, Jawaharlal Nehru, K. Kamaraj, Indira Gandhi and Lal Bahadur Shastri. He told me that he

G.K. Moopanar with other leaders

G.K. Moopanar with Dr. M.G. Ramachandran

liked it very much. After giving the "blessings packet" I said that both Krishnammal and Jegannathan were really doing good service to the poor and Dalit families in Nagapattinam

District. He asked me some questions. "Are you drawn towards them? Do you like their activities? Are you supporting them?" To all the questions I said, "Yes". Further he told me, "Palanithurai, among the living Gandhians, they are the real fighters. They have been fighting against injustice. They have no fear. They have been doing useful work for the poor. People like you should support them by way of writing and publishing about their activities." When I said, "Yes, I will try," G.K. Moopanar said, "Don't try, but do". He further explained, "It is necessary to search for good people doing good work and appreciate their services and extend support to them. Otherwise nobody will come forward to do social work." He had such a noble opinion about Gandhian workers.

10

Making Others Happy

We know pretty well that G.K. Moopanar used to make many social calls. Many politicians make such social calls. But they do so only because they will fetch support for them and for their party. But G.K. Moopanar's social calls were different. If anyone informed him of an old Congressman or a freedom fighter, he would make a visit to that house. Before visiting their houses, he never informed them. It was always a surprise visit. The person who received G.K. Moopanar would get a pleasant surprise. In the same way he would visit his contemporaries. Sometimes I felt that he was wasting his precious time, because by visiting these people, he could gain nothing. I was wondering why he was paying such social calls. One day, I put this question to him. He told me "Palanithurai, I am doing it for my satisfaction. I feel extremely happy in recognizing a person who is in need of such recognition. Moreover by my visiting them they are made happy. In human life, after all what are we going to achieve? Make others also happy. Are you losing anything? Nothing. To keep them happy I am visiting them. Beyond that there is no reason behind it." I got this reply from him long back. When I got this reply from him I could not understand its real implication. I saw many photographs of G.K. Moopanar in the houses of ordinary Congress workers. A Congress worker is interested in keeping that portrait of G.K. Moopanar in his house. Many TMC workers informed me of the visit of G.K. Moopanar to their houses even for a minor function. Some of them told me that G.K. Moopanar had his own method by which he used to visit

G.K. Moopanar with Dr. M.K. Karunanidhi

workers' houses. He used to leave his car far away from the house of the Congress worker and he walked down the whole distance whereby he gave impression that G.K. Moopanar recognized the worker. The people in the whole street used to watch the visit of G.K. Moopanar. After his visit to the house,

G.K. Moopanar with Dr. J. Jeyalalitha

G.K. Moopanar with CPI(M) Leader Shri N. Sankaraiah

G.K. Moopanar with CPI Leader Shri Nallakannu

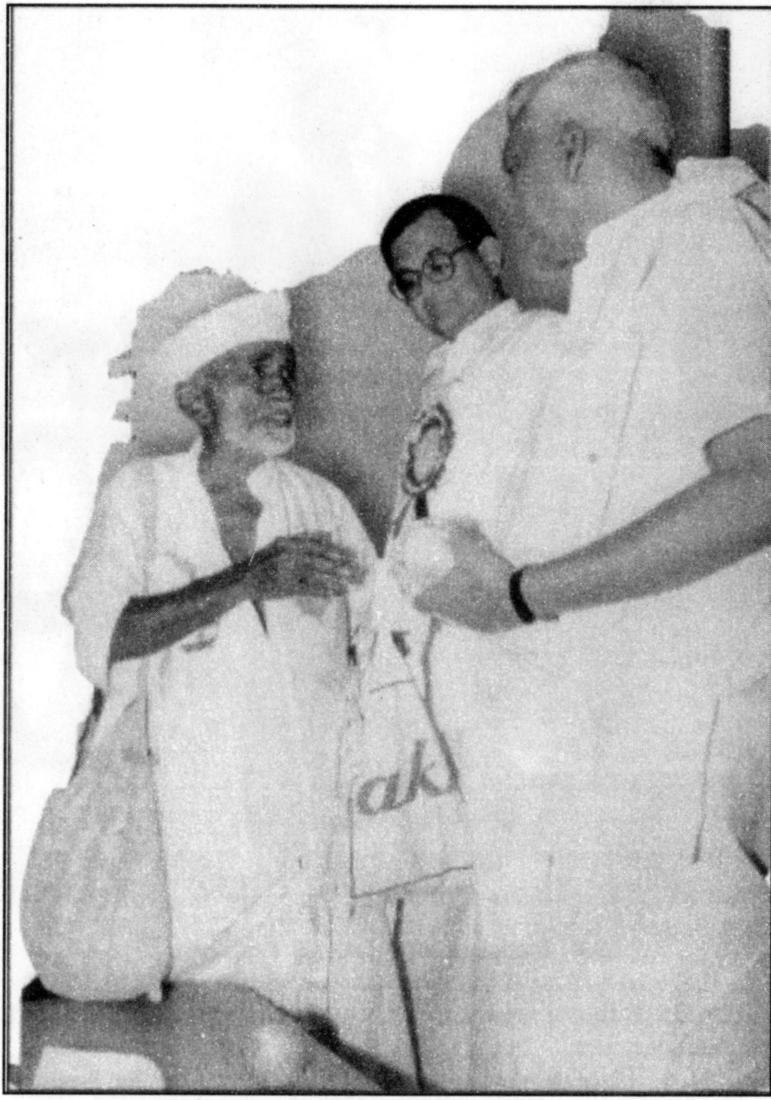

G.K. Moopanar with a Gandhian worker and Dr. P. Chidambaram

G.K. Moopanar with Thugluk Ramasamy

the image of that worker among the people in the street would be changed.

Now I got this point from Dr. Abdul Kalam, Former President of India. One journalist asked him, when he was the President of India, why he visited places and met people frequently? He said, "To make the people happy. People want happiness. My visit makes them happy. Hence I am visiting." Now I realize the value of G.K. Moopanar. For me his visit to

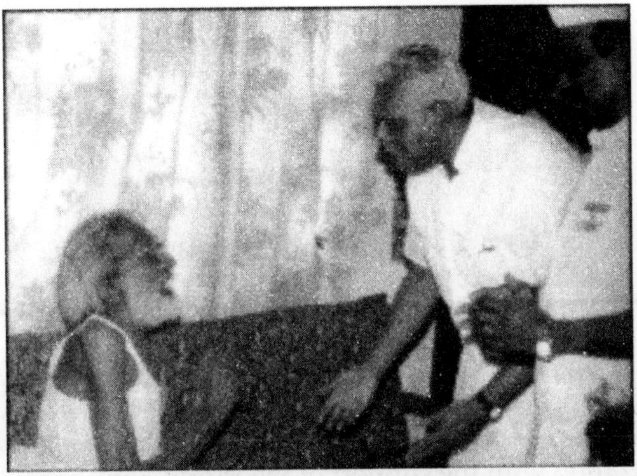

G.K. Moopanar greeting a Gandhian

the house of a freedom fighter or an old Congressman was a waste. For him it was of value. His son G.K. Vasan is doing the same thing now. Hence I no longer question such visits but I attach much value to such visits.

11

On Good Governance

When I casually met him in his office, G.K. Moopanar asked me what I presented the previous day in a meeting about which there was a report in *The Hindu*. I replied that a Development Organization with the support of the World Bank organised a workshop on 'Good Governance', that I was invited to make a presentation and that I did so.

He asked me what 'good governance' was. I gave him a definition given by the World Bank and the UNDP. He told me that our Tamil poet Thiruvalluvar has given a definition of this concept of good governance. "Are you aware of it?" he asked. I said, "Yes".

He asked me the difference between the definition of Thiruvalluvar and the World Bank. I said, "The World Bank is much worried about the money given to countries for developmental activities which are syphoned off by politicians and administrators". After listening to me he made a sarcastic comment: "When the World Bank gives money and asks us to speak about good governance, we all speak. When Kamaraj asks us to speak about good governance, we say it is politics." He further said, "It is unfortunate that our politics and administration have become corrupt and hence whoever comes to India or to poor countries, gives money and dictates terms. Look at India in the formative years of Independence. We were not rich. Our army was not so strong. Our science and technology were still developing. We did not have enough food. Yet our leaders were respected. Their leadership had credibility and acceptability. The whole world looked for views from Jawaharlal Nehru. Our leaders had moral worth. Look at

G.K. Moopanar reading newspaper

today. We have a strong economy. Our economy is a fast growing economy. Yet our leaders are not respected. And no one looks for India's views. Because we have lost our credibility and credential. What we need today is good leadership. That is the need of the hour." It was a good analysis made by him. He listed a number of leaders who were known for their credibility, efficiency, and honesty. They led a simple life. They maintained the rule of law. But now where is such rule of law? These leaders were at both the national level and the state level. "What they did as politicians, as administrators, about good governance. They were simple, people-friendly, humane, and selfless. All their activities were people-centric, development-centric and more particularly poor-centric. They might not have given much advertisement about their work and sacrifices but they provided good governance. Who bothers about it? If you tell the story, the people, that too youngsters, will not believe you. Even Einstein made such a great observation about Gandhi." After the above observation, I asked, "Why were the lives of such honest leaders not recorded and documented?" He said it is the style of the functioning of the Congress. It was time for his lunch. I took leave of him.

12

On Rajinikanth

There is yet another conversation we had on Rajinikanth. He asked me about the future role of Rajinikanth in Tamil Nadu politics. I immediately replied that I would produce a report after a month. I instructed some of my students and researchers to conduct a survey during the holidays. A sample survey was conducted. I prepared a report and gave it to him. I have incorporated that report in my book, which was published later by MD Publications, New Delhi. Based on the survey I informed G.K. Moopanar that 80 per cent of the Rajinikanth's fans wanted Rajinikanth to be involved in politics directly. In the event of this not taking place, the fans would move towards the Tamil Maanila Congress. Moving towards the Tamil Maanila Congress has already started. Many of Rajinikanth's fans have already joined the Tamil Maanila Congress. They are to be oriented and retained. I further informed that if the Tamil Maanila Congress is able to take steps to accommodate the Rajini's fans fully, the party will be strengthened. It is to be noted that the Tamil Maanila Congress has to move on a totally different path to accommodate the fans of Rajinikanth. If it follows the path of the Indian National Congress, the TMC cannot attract the youths to its fold. If it gives serious attention to this, it has got tremendous potential to draw more youth into the fold of the TMC. By doing so the party will reach new heights. Moreover, Rajinikanth, given his nature, will not organise a political party in Tamil Nadu in the near future. He moves step by step and in a calculated way. There is a gap between his fans and him on their political perceptions. Unless

G.K. Moopanar with Actor Rajinikanth

they are ironed out, there will not be any possibility for him to form a new political party. Hence he will not take such a risk. This was the content of the report. Further, he asked me a question about the value profile developed by Rajinikanth. In fact Rajini talks much about values. But the youth are moving towards him as fans and pressurizing him to start a political party with the aim of capturing power as MGR did. I informed him that there is a gap between the intention of Rajini and his fans in terms of adopting a value profile. In this context Rajinikanth coming to politics is a remote possibility. When I made this observation G.K. Moopanar intervened and said that Rajinikanth is a highly value based man and hence he will ask his followers to follow the value profile. It will be good because the political culture of the state will be changed by this process. Definitely it will be a welcome change. This was the observation of G.K. Moopanar about Rajinikanth. He held Rajinikanth in high esteem. But I made it clear that Rajinikanth's political entry will be distant and not in the near future.

After listening to me he asked me another question: "Some people suggested that the Tamil Maanila Congress should have contested in the election 'with the support of Rajnikanth' instead of aligning with the DMK. Is it the correct perspective?"

I responded that it was correct in one sense. People perceived that it was a wave at that time. You could have taken the risk. In all probability, the Tamil Maanila Congress could have won the election. After the election the Tamil Maanila Congress could have consolidated and stabilized its position. This was the proposal and dream of many. It was also one of the options perceived at that point of time. Then he said, "It was a good dream". "The dream could have been realized if you had taken the risk" was my observation. He stared at me. Then I left the place after taking his permission.

13

An Alternative Approach

I met G.K. Moopanar in Vedaranayam, Kanya Kurukulam and later in a meeting organized by P.V. Rajendran, Former M.P. of Mayiladuthurai. Behind the stage (dais), there was a small cabin for relaxing, when I was on the dais I was asked to go with G.K. Moopanar to the small cabin where tender coconut was served. G.K. Moopanar asked me what was the alternative to be projected now in Tamil Nadu politics? This was based on my suggestion to him long back in a conversation. I could not recollect immediately what I had said then. But gradually I recollected it and explained to him that it was nothing but suggesting an alternative approach for development of Tamil Nadu.

It had to do with how the Tamil Maanila Congress is going to perform and what strategy it has, to achieve development in Tamil Nadu. In every activity, the Tamil Maanila Congress has to demonstrate that it is unique. Such a perception has to be created among the people. Even the conduct of party meetings and the approach of the party leaders and workers have to be different from that of the DMK and the AIADMK. People should feel that the TMC is different and really it is an alternative. When I mentioned all the details, G.K. Moopanar intervened and asked me to give a few examples. I said that if it is a party activity, it should be organized without pomp and show. It should be very simple and inexpensive. "Even when you serve food for any event, the food should be very simple. In the same way, simple accommodation has to be arranged. People should feel that these great leaders are leading a simple life. The existing cinematic show culture has to be changed."

Supposing the Government is introducing the budget, the party should comment on the budget by introducing its own budget. The TMC has to highlight the advantages of the budget of the TMC. Likewise when policies are announced, they are to be critiqued by evolving alternative policies. Intellectuals have to be involved in party activities for preparation of alternative budget and alternative policy papers. Periodically party MLAs have to be oriented in legislative proceedings. All legislative nuances have to be used to project the issues of the people. Members of the Legislative Assembly should know how to review a policy and to suggest ways and means to improve the policies. In the same way, the members should be in a position to understand how to aggregate the demands of the people of the constituency and articulate them in the Legislative Assembly. By the performance of the members of the Legislative Assembly, a new legislative culture could be

created. Even the Legislative Assembly can be reformed. To perform the above, series of exercises are needed. Rigorous training is to be imparted. The TMC can attempt such a kind of venture. The party should give a perception to the people that the TMC has got good, committed legislators with a high intellectual orientation. There are retired IAS officials, retired academics and media persons willing to help the TMC. They can be used for this kind of exercise. When I made all these points, he reacted sharply, "All your suggestions are different from the current culture. They require a different attitude, behaviour and performance, on the part of the leaders and the cadres. We can try and there is nothing wrong in it." He told me that these are all good ideas but asked who will take all these ideas seriously and translate them into reality in the party. "Let us try", was his response. Then he moved to the dias.

After a few days, I saw a news item in *The Hindu* pertaining to his views on a policy matter where he mentioned that the TMC is going to prepare alternative policy papers but subsequently, I did not heard anything. I asked myself why some of the good thoughts nurtured by the leaders are not translated into action? There may be a gap between the leader and the second level leaders in the party.

APPENDIX I

Rejuvenating the Congress Party

G.K. Moopanar asked me to develop a framework to develop the TMC party and I submitted a draft to him. On receipt he appreciated me and he gave it to few party functionaries. No action was taken on this draft. Now it is applicable to the Indian National Congress. Hence it is given here.

Background

India is always a wonder to many. Nowhere does one find such extreme variations, differences and diversities and yet we are keeping democracy alive and vibrant. Many theories evolved from the western experience have been disproved in India. Hence understanding India is not an easy task. It requires a very deep analysis.

Indian society is undergoing a change and it is being fragmented very quickly as the market forces are affecting the society very deeply. Everyone wants democracy and equally every one wants prosperity and development. Collectivities, which are having the needed skill, capacity and capability and access to credit, make use of the new opportunities and achieve prosperity. The present democratic governance helps them acquire such a kind of prosperity. They are comfortable and positive towards the existing order, arrangement of administration and governance. Another set of people are having same aspirations for prosperity but they could not achieve it and, as a result they develop a negative feeling and perception towards the existing institutional mechanisms. They agitate against the system as they are in democracy. Every segment in India today wants development and compares itself with the other social segments through their identities. They are being mobilized by the political parties and are being used intensively for their political advantage. Media and research institutions provide authentic reports about the position, status and conditions of the marginalized and neglected communities for their understanding and internalization. Many agencies in India are working towards creating awareness among the deprived sections about their status and position. To some extent, people have come out from self-pity and started asserting themselves as stakeholders. Over a period of time political parties have raised hopes among the people in terms of material benefits individually and collectively and by which people are mobilized with different identities in the name of religion, culture, language, region and caste. Now, people are having multiple identities and they are used profitably for their own advantage.

As identities for mobilization of people are accepted as social mobilization for emancipation, people are continuously mobilized. But mobilization on the basis of religion is considered as fundamentalism and it is a threat to secularism. No doubt, like the other identities religion also stirs emotive feelings among the people and hence it is being used powerfully and forcefully. Secularism is western and is not known to the people. Ordinary citizens do not appreciate the concept of secularism. Hence Mahatma Gandhi used the term 'inter-religious' communal harmony and not 'secularism'. People are not communal and communities are not communal and unless they are oriented communally, communities will have a common understanding and develop a habit of respecting each other. Unfortunately, these cards are being played by politicians for preparing people emotively to achieve their political ends.

In sixty years of governance, India has not increased the people's faith in the governing and the administrative system. Day by day they are loosing hope in the present system. Since they have no other alternative they remain in the representative democracy. People who are on the periphery, have come to conclusion that they cannot come out from poverty and they continue to be in the poverty trap. As a result one can see the extreme mistrust and conflict among the social collectivities.

Regional political parties, sub-regional parties and smaller identity-based political parties have emerged in India by using the crises in politics, society and economics and ultimately reduced the space of the national political parties. National political parties do not have vibrant ideological framework and especially they do not address the issues of disparities among the communities, and regions and hence they are not able to bring the small parties into their fold on ideological ground. The political parties are coming together not under the framework of ideology. It is always a marriage of convenience. It is easier for the smaller political parties to move from one group to another by citing the reasons which are advantageous to their cadres. Now the emergence of sub-regional political parties and caste-based political parties has reduced the space of regional and ethnic political parties. By securing a few seats in the Parliament and Legislative Assembly within the region they have became powerful at the national level. This syndrome has spread to many states. Hence coalitions are formed at the state level also. No one gets an absolute majority. As a result, national level coalition and state level coalition governments have been formed. Coalition governments initially broke down and but now they are maturing. Over a period of time rules of the game will be evolved.

Further the space of politics and office of service have been converted into space and office of profit. Totally politics has been converted into a business proposal and it is made known to people also through their activities. It is always a 'win win' situation for everyone. By joining politics whether you win in the election or not, you are not going to loose money. One will gain money. Politics has been shaped in Tamil Nadu in this manner.

In this context, the national political parties want to strengthen their base and try to come out from the coalition arrangement which is not conducive either for the development of this country or the party. Moreover, both are mutually opposed and contradictory. The activities of the coalition partners will affect the major player in the coalition and the activities of the major player will affect the partners of the coalition. In the states the major partner in the national coalition has less space and expansion possibility is reduced as the major coalition partner in the state has to play the second fiddle. In the same way the state coalition arrangement provides less scope for the minor partners for expansion as more number of players are competing with each other for the same space.

There are regional political parties, and caste-based political parties which have limited area of operations. They have vote banks and accordingly bargain with the major players and secure a number of seats commensurate with their strength. But the issues of development and governance are increasing in society which must get the attention of the political parties. The aspirations of the people are also increasing. Because of competitive populism, people are oriented to demand more and more from the government. Thus a new situation has emerged. Almost all the parties have moved over to new terrain from the original perspectives and basic issues. The issues left over by some of the political parties in the new context have been captured by the new parties which have acted on them from different perspective. Moreover, the modern political parties are emerging like corporate companies. The policy of *quid pro quo* will work very effectively and hence people join in the new political parties not with the hope of good governance. They want to share in the spoils if their party comes to power. This results in political mobilization. A profit seeking approach has been developed. "Make money from politics and strengthen the party and through party serve the cadres". It is the company approach. Once people used to say that it is good to "serve and suffer". Now the message is "serve and prosper".

Against this background, one has to visualize the development of the Indian National Congress. The Indian National Congress has receded from the grassroots and it is strong in certain pockets only. The other parties have developed a practice of establishing client pattern relationship and, as a result, the party which comes to power distributes spoils to the party men and hence party men work with the aim of getting profit when their party succeeds in the elections. Every party needs a leader who can deliver the goods. In the Indian context, a charismatic leader can well develop his party and capture power. However, his party should have a sound organizational structure from the head office to the party units in each and every Gram Panchayat area. A party cannot win elections based on the leader alone. A charismatic leader can pull the crowd but he cannot convert the masses into voters unless they are shaped by the party units in every Panchayat area. In each Gram Panchayat, one has to find a person to look after the party and another one or two or three persons to serve as booth agents for the party. They are the strong party units on the ground. They are to be oriented. The regional political parties and sub-regional political parties are well organized in this respect down to the grassroots. The national political parties are not having such a kind of structure and approach.

Now-a-days, in order to orient the cadres and to ensure party loyalty, the party leaders' photographs are being inserted in rings. The party functionaries have to wear cloths like the party leaders. Each and every political party has its own dress code. They are mobilized for political action continuously. Party cadres are engaged fully in the political activities. Everything should be done professionally. Now the Indian National Congress Party has been forced to go to the regional political parties to get their support for the formation of a coalition governments and for its sustenance. For the emerging political parties both at the national and regional level, it is understandable that they have to go to the other parties to get their support in their efforts to capture power. But the Indian National Congress has been a ruling party for several decades. How did it lose its space to the regional and sub-regional political parties? It is a major question. Basically the Indian National Congress emerged as a result of a movement. It was a national liberation movement, a platform for all political parties to record their voices. Now it has been reduced to a level where the party has been made to listen to the partners always and to act according to the demands of its allies. How and why did the Indian National Congress come to this stage, reduced to this level?

It is a well known fact that the leaders of the Indian National Congress really managed the people through their charisma, especially at the dawn of Independence. Their intensions were good and yet why the Indian National Congress has failed to consolidate the masses under its fold despite the fact that the party ruled the country for a long. Somewhere the Indian National Congress drifted and failed to cope with the rising aspirations of the people. At the dawn of Independence, all political leaders gave the hope that the leaders would work for the poor and for the emancipation of the marginalized. Their life style was always simple and they worked hard without wasting public money. But now it is totally different and to run a political party and contest in the elections both the parties and the candidates are in need of money. So the whole political system has been reduced to a corrupt one. Is there any scope for the Indian National Congress to reinvent itself and expand its base all over the country. Do we find vibrant leaders to strengthen the party at present both at the centre and in the states? What are the strategies to be followed?.

Before observations based on analysis one has to understand the context and its implications. The present era is a market era. Everything is determined on the basis of the profit in the market. No one believes that politicians are honest and administrators are honest. People have developed a perception based on their experience that the whole system of governance and administration has become corrupt, not friendly towards the people. The political parties have given an image that politics fetches huge money for which one has to join in a party which is likely to become a ruling party or a party of the ruling alliance. It encourages individuals to join political parties on the basis of the profit proposition. The political parties have developed themselves like the corporate sector. If a company fetches profit, your salary and other perks will be enhanced. Likewise, if your party comes to power, you can get the spoils.

In this context, the position and problems of the Indian National Congress have to be analysed. The Congress Party is full of rulers in the guise of leaders. They want Sonia Gandhi's face, Rahul Gandhi's face, Priyanka's face to get votes. But they are not willing to work in tune with the times. Everyone has to go to the villages and not to New Delhi. Leaders have to give messages that workers will be respected and they will be given due recognition. For recognizing the services of the workers, tickets have to be issued to the workers for Legislative Assembly elections and Parliament elections. A worker should not get an impression that tickets are issued on the basis of recommendation of some central leaders. At present, people are economically rational. The Congress has slowly receded and given more space to the regional political parties as the regional political parties have used the regional card, language card, caste card. But without evolving a strategy to combat these forces, the Congress has struck to the old position and, as a result, regional political parties have gained power. Leaders in Congress consider themselves to be bigger than the party. Internal fighting is common in all political parties. But when external enemies approach, there is no infight in the regional parties. The Indian National Congress is the only party which continues to fight even during times of external threats.

In Tamil Nadu, K. Kamaraj, a national leader worked in the region and showed the way for the whole of the country. Kamaraj evolved a model of development. Even for politics he developed a model. He provided opportunities for the aspirations of the middle classes, marginalized classes and backward classes. He worked hard to induct more number of representatives from all backward classes and Dalits. He predicted that the polarization in politics and society would take place on the basis of caste and class. Hence, he tried to accommodate all the sections. Further, he wanted the party leaders to lead a simple life style and by which he kept them closer to the people.

He introduced reservation for OBC people in education and employment. He made a Dalit the Minister for Hindu Religious Endowments Department. He introduced the Noon

Meal Scheme. These were all flagship programmes. E.V. Ramasamy Periyar, who came out of the Congress Party after accusing the Congress that of being a Brahmin party, appreciated K. Kamaraj. Even when the Congress was defeated in 1967, it had been polled one per cent more votes than what the DMK got. K. Kamaraj provided opportunity for the middle and the lower middle class in the party to emerge as leaders. The Congress was feudal when K. Kamaraj was the Chief Minister in Tamil Nadu. But, he enabled many from the last rung of the society to become leaders. Now no feudal lord can attract the masses. But, in other provinces, we find the Congress leaders containing to be feudal and that image has to be changed. It should become a common man's party. All political parties create literature on the achievements of the party by commissioning studies. But Congress has a track record which is taken for granted by everyone. Books have to be written on the activities and achievements of the Congress and the Congress leaders from 1952 to 1967. This will enable the party cadres to understand the track of the party.

For party cadres, identity is an imperative. Their identification with the party, party symbols, party leaders, party goals and party attire are important. All political parties are orienting their party cadres in all these aspects. In the Congress party even prominent leaders do not wear khadi attire. The whole life style has to be changed. Congressmen and women are not oriented. Very rarely meetings are organized for party workers. There is no regional executive and there is no regional general council meetings. As long as these meetings are not conducted, there won't be any party cadre. One will find group loyalists and they will go with their group leaders and not with the party. This is a very serious issue affecting the party. Even parties having 5 per cent votes are convening such meetings and they are covered by the press. In Tamil Nadu the Congressmen and women are found in Railway Stations and Airports to receive their group leaders but not to receive the TNCC President. There are Gram Panchayat Presidents from the Congress Party. But the TNCC President is not aware of the Gram Panchayat Presidents who belong to the Congress Party. All political parties are orienting their Local Body leaders. But the TNCC never tried to organize any such meet on the Local Bodies. It has given a perception to the workers that workers cannot gain anything. Only persons who can go to New Delhi will get benefits in the party. The following steps must be taken to strengthen the Congress Party in Tamil Nadu:

- Group politics will end only if an elected leader is in position for a specific period.
- The party should have a pucca office with all paraphernalia in the State. Just like a company it has to have district headquarter offices with required facilities.
- The party should have wing leaders such as for women, Dalits, Local Bodies, minorities, farmers, workers and so on. All these positions have to be created and filled.
- A party should own a newspaper but it should be run by a small group of independent people under a trust run by the party.
- A party should have a Television Channel and it should also be given into the hands of a few attached to the trust.
- A party should have think tanks with a team of intellectuals. They need not necessarily be the members of the party. All issues should be discussed here. Opinions can be generated from them. In Chennai alone there are around 270 retired civil servants. Of them many are willing to help those who are in need of their service. Already some of the parties are using this intellectual power.
- The party should have a documentation centre and library. The TNCC does not have a sense of history and hence it does not maintain a pucca documentation centre.
- All party leaders—from the state level to village level—names and other details of the leaders should be gathered and available on line.

- In the party headquarters, building a good library is an imperative need.
- The party trust has to be effectively managed and it should help the party leaders to be trained. It should be a training institute. It should have a publication division. It should have a documentation division.
- Connectivity has to be created from the party office from New Delhi to State Capital, State Capital to district headquarters and district headquarters to villages. A digitalized system has to be created.
- Party cadres have to be engaged through activities whether the party is in power or not. They should be engaged continuously as it is done by the Communists, the PMK, DMK and AIADMK.
- Party leaders and cadres must wear khadi.
- In all 12689 Gram Panchayat areas, the party flag should be hoisted.
- Party cadres have to be oriented to read the party newspaper.
- Party cadres should be trained to work as a liaison between the people and the government.
- In every Gram Panchayat, there should be a party unit. The unit has to be led by a leader with a small committee including booth agents.
- In every Block Panchayat area, there should be a unit which should be vibrant. A permanent office with all the needed facilities should be created.
- In every district, there should be a unit for party. It should be active. A fixed office preferably in its own building should be created.
- Collective leadership is the need of the hour. Develop collective leadership in the party.
- All celebrations have to be conducted periodically by the party.
- All party functions should be conducted in a very simple way.

- Executive meetings, General Council Meetings have to be conducted in different places, preferably in different district headquarters.
- Membership fee has to be collected from the cadres. It should not be paid by some individuals alone.
- Rahul Gandhi's new scheme to attract the youth can be started in Tamil Nadu to put an end to group politics. Four or five visits by Rahul Gandhi will change the scenario by mobilizing youth for the party in Tamil Nadu.

APPENDIX II

Drifting Away from the Path Shown by Mahatma Gandhi

[This is based on article written by the late K. Kamaraj in *Ananda Vikatan* (A Tamil Weekly Magazine—Special Issue for Deepavali) during the centenary celebrations of Mahatma Gandhi in the year 1969]

The centenary celebration of Mahatma Gandhi has come during a period of acute turmoil, conflict among communities, conflict over fundamentalism and intense hatred among people and collectivities. In a way the present darkness will bring light by remembering the thoughts and actions of Mahatma Gandhi by the people of India. We have to raise a question whether we follow the path of Mahatma Gandhi. If not, at least we can correct ourselves by now and move into the proper track with courage and conviction for which this is considered as a fine opportunity. No doubt in the last two decades after Independence we have made tremendous progress in the field of industry and education and we can be proud of these achievements. At the same time we have a fear whether deeply entrenched moral and ethical values are shaken. There is no advantage in hiding this truth.

In the process of achieving a goal at a great speed it is natural that we commit mistakes. But the mistakes have to be corrected immediately. If we are not concerned about the mistakes committed by us, we tend to commit more mistakes continuously and finally, we have to meet failure in achieving our goal. Along with that we tend to give our heart for petty things by which the values we have evolved, cherished and practiced will be spoiled. That is why Mahatma Gandhi not only fixed the goal but also showed the means by which one can reach the goal. Means and ends are equally important. It is not enough to have lofty ideas and goals. The means by which we reach the goals is more important than the ends. He emphasized the above in unequivocal terms. He himself was a model practitioner.

He led the freedom struggle in a non-violent way. When there was mass upsurge in violent forms against his wishes and principles, he inflicted punishment on himself. By observing fasts he indicated to the people that they were drifting away from the chosen path. When people indulged in violent activities in Chowri Chowra, he stopped his struggle against the British. C.R. Dass, Motilal Nehru and other leaders opposed the decision of Gandhi and yet Gandhi did not change his decision.

The poor repose faith in the system of governance despite India is a country facing severe poverty. It will remain a democratic country where the poor can enjoy freedom. That is why Mahatma Gandhi identified himself with the poor. The poor should feel that they are in a democracy, and they can also enjoy freedom. The poor men's instrument, the *charkha* became an instrument for Mahatma Gandhi, despite their positions and intellectual calibre, the leaders started living a simple life forgetting their status. They demonstrated that a simple life is possible and everyone can lead simple life. Motilal Nehru, C.R. Dass, Jawaharlal Nehru, Rajendra Prasad, Rajaji and others had led simple lives by abjuring luxury and comfort.

By leading a simple life and aligning himself with the common man Mahatma Gandhi gave a hope to the people that the goal would be achieved. People reposed faith in the leaders and the goal. The simplicity of the leaders, and their dedication motivated the people. Every Indian, despite his poverty, was enthusiastic in keeping the high moral standards in life. Today it is sad to note that the ethical and moral turpitude holds sway. The leaders who proclaim that they were leading the society today are responsible for the fall of moral standards as their life pattern and behaviour have changed. During the period of Mahatma Gandhi, no worker in the freedom movement travelled in the higher class on trains. What is the position today? The person who addresses the issue of economic inequalities and the ways and means by which they can be tackled, travels in a luxury car, after delivering his speech in the public meeting. When the people look at all these contradictions, will they believe our leaders or the ideas mooted by the leaders? A car is essential today. But one has to travel based on the need. But in reality, the leaders are using cars in terms of their status. The quality of the car is decided upon by the level of the position he or she enjoys. It is a display of power and of position.

It is not so easy to wipe out economic inequalities. It will take time. To achieve the goal of attacking the economic inequalities, the leaders who are working for it have to lead a life like the poor. Then only people will feel that these leaders can relieve them from the shackles of poverty. They will also feel that they can wait for some more time as the leaders are also in the struggle to mitigate poverty and reduce inequality. People make declarations that they will work for the poor, to mitigate their sufferings. But they lead a luxurious life. Will the people have faith in such leaders? People will think that achieving equality is only a talk and not a reality.

Unfortunately today we witness this type of contradictions. Not only that, this contradiction has increased. Faith in pomp and show, aspirations in capturing positions and to do anything for capturing positions and to retain the captured positions have increased. As a result moral standards have gone down. It is a danger to our democracy also. Mahatma Gandhi did not show these paths to us. Such contradictions seen in higher places will spoil the future generations. To redeem the country from these dangers, people who have faith in Mahatma Gandhi must take up responsibility with a sense of commitment, dedication, courage and conviction even if they have to face difficulties. People who are drifting away from the main path have to be brought into the mainstream for which one has to struggle. If we allow the country to forget its moral values, we cannot succeed in our onward march to reach our goals. Hence at least a few have to work boldly and courageously for upholding moral values in public life. It is the best tribute one can pay to Mahatma Gandhi.

APPENDIX III

Do away with Corruption and Caste System

G.K. Moopanar

[An article published (in Tamil) during the Fiftieth Anniversary celebration of our Independence in *Dinamani* (A Tamil Newspaper) Golden Jubilee volume]

In 1947, I was 16, studying in Jawahar Board High School in Papanasam in Tanjore District of Tamil Nadu. I was in the 10th Standard (5th Form). Three months before Independence everywhere freedom of our country was the talk of the street.

Even inside the campus of the school if three or four students joined together, Gandhi, Nehru, Congress leaders, Independence Day celebration were the topics of discussion.

My maternal uncle Palanisamy Moopanar was an ardent Congressman. He was a member of the District Council. He was a regular khadi wearer and attended a series of meetings. He always used to discuss with his friends the independence movement and the activities of the Congressmen.

One Mr. Manicka Mudaliar, a veteran Freedom Fighter was in our village. He was the leader of all the activities of the Indian National Congress. He was responsible for some of the party activities in our area.

His holding in his hand the national tricolour flag and shouting slogan like 'Mahatma Gandhi ki Jay', 'Vandematram' in the remote interior village setting is still ringing in my years. With a khadi cap on his head his moving image is indelible in my memory.

Why he undertook such a kind of struggle was not clear to me. When he was arrested and taken to prison the whole village talked about him. He belonged to the Senguntha Mudaliar community. He was a respected person in our village. He used to come to meet my maternal uncle. When he came to our uncle's house to meet him, we used to look at him with respect and awe.

On the day of Independence in our village, through a loud speaker Bharati's song "All will sing that we got Independence" was on the air throughout the village. All the streets were decorated with coloured festoons. Before every house rangoli was drawn. The tricolour national flag was hoisted in many places in the village. Everywhere slogans were raised to praise Mahatma Gandhi. Everyone was emotionally charged. I did not have an opportunity to participate directly in the freedom struggle. Even though I was not fully aware what freedom was and what for freedom was needed, one thing was clear that we were freed from the colonial yoke. This filled the heart of everyone with joy. I could not forget the joy which everyone had on that day.

Time has passed smoothly. Fifty years have gone by after Independence. How swiftly they have gone by is really a surprise. I never thought that I would involve myself and play a significant role in the Indian National Congress and the politics of India and more particularly in Tamil Nadu.

Poondi (name of a place in Tanjore District) Thiru Krishnasamy Vandaiyar was our family friend. He was close to my father. He was the President of the District Congress Committee. He was the person who introduced me to Kamaraj.

When I met Perunthalaivar (K. Kamaraj) first I felt that I was blessed to have contacted him by divine grace. I had such a feeling on the day of my meeting with him.

I had a feeling as if someone said that the leader I was searching for was there. From that day onwards my contact with him and respect for and faith in him increased and finally, I became part of his political life. It was a rare gift I gained in my life.

Whenever I thought of Annai Indira Gandhi, and young leader Rajiv Gandhi, my heart was filled with joy and extreme happiness. The work done under their leadership is still in my memory and it cannot be erased easily from my memory.

Just like the rose which spreads fragrance even after it dried up, the death of the two great leaders was a personal loss to me. Even after a long period I cannot forget them. Their killings has left deep scars.

The Tamil Maanila Congress was an unexpected turning point in my political life which I had never expected. I never had any joy when I came out from the Congress Party, in which I had served forty years without expecting anything from it.

I had a strong belief that the weakening of the Congress Party will weaken the whole country. I was sure about this proposition. But when the Congress went ahead to forge an alliance with a corrupt regime I was not prepared to accept it. Having decided not to go with the corrupt regime I decided to keep away from it.

But the whole of Tamil Nadu, Tamil Nadu Congress and lakhs and lakhs of Congress workers expected leadership from me. When I perceived the expectations of the Congress workers, I did not want to escape from that responsibility. When the country celebrated the Golden Jubilee of our Independence the Tamil Maanila Congress wanted to wipe out the roots of a corrupt regime. It acted as an instrument to accomplish that task. I had the full satisfaction that we had worked for a just cause.

When the nation was celebrating the Golden Jubilee of our Independence we could not say that we had not achieved anything in the past. If anybody said so, I won't accept it. Our achievements in economy, industrial development, agriculture in rural areas, education, science and technology were impressive.

When we felt proud of all these achievements, I could not set aside my apprehension and anguish over the events happening in India. The Prime Minister of India I.K. Gujral made a statement about what was going on in India was really jolted out of her own beliefs and faiths. "Our country is immersed in corruption", was the observation of the then Prime Minister. It drew the attention of all. The deeply entrenched corruption in public life would destabilise our democracy. Our democracy would die soon. Our unity and integrity would not be maintained without representative democracy.

Eradication of corruption was just like another war of independence. It had to emerge as a people's movement. That was the only way of salvation to India. Corruption endangers the very future of India and caste jeopardizes and question the very future of Tamil Nadu. When I saw the caste feelings, caste animosity and caste conflicts I was terribly disturbed. Tamil Nadu should not encourage those elements which use caste as a force and instrument to mobilize the people for votes.

Twenty-five years before India got Independence, Bharathi a National Poet of India, had composed a poem in which he posed questions as if raised by the British officials to the Indians who demanded freedom and Independence. It reads thus:

> "You are the servants and slaves to do service
> Do you have thoughts of Freedom?
> Have you ever seen or felt it?
> Do you deserve it?
> Has your caste conflict gone?
> Has your conflict on religion gone?
> Now you have come demanding justice
> Don't stand before me
> Have you learnt to live in unity?
> Does the slave have the strength?
> Will you live together?
> Will you destroy your petty characters and feelings?
> To protect your country
> Do you have any knowledge?
> Go and protect the houses
> Slave, Go for work".

APPENDIX IV

Monarchs in Democracy*

C.N. Annadurai

Nobody can question and nobody can stop a man's activities when he is made a king and, as a result, he never feels for his atrocities committed on the people. He has no fear. At his command he has an army to suppress the poor and the rural folk when they oppose him. Hence the reason for atrocities being committed on the people is not that a bad man becomes the king but the system of monarchy itself. Monarchy breeds such a kind of atrocities against the people. Hence people felt that monarchy is not needed. So, a system by of controllable and accountable governance was created. It should be formed by us and dissolvable by us and, at the same time, we should not be discriminated against in the ruling arrangement and establishment. This was the belief system which came into the minds of the people and thus democracy came into existence.

The concept of a king ruling has gone. A person has been chosen to lead the society. It is people who give power to the persons who govern us. It is democracy. It is representative democracy. "They are my subjects," has gone but "they are our representatives to govern us" has come. "I say" of the monarch has gone and "we approve" has come. It is a system born in the world. The rulers are not in the palaces but in the work spots. The concept of "God has given power to rule" has gone. "You have given us opportunities to govern" has come. "I am the king, because my father was also a king. I am the king, hence my son will become a king". This statement has no

---

* It was written in 1965.

more relevance today. We extended support and hence he is governing now. We can select yet another candidate for governance. Now it has become a reality.

It is a long journey. It took a long time. There were many restrictions and hurdles in this process. There is a heavy loss. When they reach the stage of establishing democracy the journey of governance starts. People begin to feel secure and they develop the faith that there won't be any atrocities against them.

The monarchy came to an end. But the possibility of committing atrocities against the people has not gone. Democracy does not proclaim that the possibility to commit atrocities has gone. The existing conditions are amply demonstrating this truth.

When monarchy was in force, the king started commanding people and acted heavily against the people. But, in democracy, the people's representatives, by their benevolent behaviour, attract the people but, through cunning devices, they will deceive the people. The king is a tiger always roaring but the representatives of the people are the snakes that kill the people stealthily.

People thought that they cannot do anything against the king. But, in a democracy, they think that the representatives of the people will continue in power as long as the people allow. Hence people live their lives without monitoring what their representatives are doing.

"I proclaim, I order, you accept what I declare". This was the statement of the king. "Order me, I will serve, I expect your order" is the statement of the representatives of the people in a representative democracy. The representatives have used democracy as an instrument to deceive people. In monarchy, the king, by his command did everything. But, in a democracy, our people's representatives, by their design and strategy, complete their work for their own advantage.

Whether it is democracy or monarchy, the dominant section deceives the people. The innocent and the ignorant are exploited. The atrocities committed against people have taken different forms today in the representative democracy.

Atrocities on the poor and exploitation of the poor have not gone. When people were unable to bear the torture and atrocities of the kings they attacked them. They revolted against the king, destroyed the palaces and killed the ruling clan. But in a democracy it is not necessary.

In monarchy it is not only the king, the whole clan and family have to be eliminated. Then only the atrocities will end. But, in a democracy, people need not do anything against the representatives as they can select another person for governance if the representatives are not reasonable and responsible.

This kind of belief has increased the self-confidence of the people. It is all right if all decisions are taken by the people. But if the people are complacent atrocities will be perpetuated. The representative democracy has created this kind of feeling among the people. People's representatives will exploit the complacent tendencies of the people.

The monarchs capitalized on the feelings of the people that the king was the representative of God to rule the country. Our people and our representatives are good and capable and they get our mandate and they will do good things for us. This is the perception developed by the people which is being used by the people's representatives. In the monarchy the king used to visit his kingdom and the people venerated the king. While the representatives visit their constituency, the entire place is decorated and the community comes to a celebration mood. People respect them and worship them. "Show us the way, we will follow you" is the slogan of the representatives.

To that level the representatives of the people instill feelings and emotions among the people by which even the monarch would envy them if he were alive. To that extent the representatives establish their sway over the people.

The representatives convince the people that they are always doing good things for them and that they stand for them. The representatives of the people commit atrocities against the people more than the atrocities committed by the king during the monarchical days. Hence, we should protect the representative democracy from being abused by the representatives. The representatives will become the elected monarchs if the system is not protected. To prevent this, the people need more awareness. Further, they need more courage and clear vision. People should not feel that they have elected their representatives who will do everything for them. We have to watch whether our representatives are performing their roles and discharging their responsibilities properly.

When they come again during elections, the people should be in a position to evaluate their performance. Based on their performance people should have the courage to reject them.

People should not fall prey to castes in order to get petty benefits. It requires a lot of conviction, clarity, commitment and courage. Citizens have to understand and carefully watch where the country is going. They should evaluate events and issues. They should keep an eye on the government. They should also know what type of government they want. Bringing about this kind of practice, attitude and activities is not so easy. All cannot get it. It cannot be gained all of a sudden. Yet, people have to acquire that kind of practice. Otherwise, people will be under the yoke of the representatives as captives. It requires more courage and conviction to remove the elected representatives from power than to dethrone a king. That is why all political pundits argue that the representative democracy is not only an instrument of governance but also a part of the culture of the society. The representative democracy has to be nurtured and fostered. It forms a part of the broader culture of the society.

The candidates contesting in the elections come with promises and with folded hands and, once the elections are over, the people have to go to the place where they live to represent their problems. People have a short memory and hence they forget everything. That is why the elected representatives are behaving irresponsibly.

The candidates who contest in the elections will hear the people but, after the elections, people have to hear what the representatives say. If democracy has to succeed, people should have power and capacity to protect the system. Hence, the capacity of the citizens has to be enhanced. The elected representatives should be monitored and their performance should be evaluated, so that the elected representatives will not sit on the heads and shoulders of the common people.

When they contest in the elections, they show their humility before the people, but, after the elections, they show scant respect for the people. People believe their representatives. But the representatives of the people believe that the public memory is short and hence the people can be deceived easily.

For the success of democracy, people have to act decisively. The candidates who come to the people before the elections are likely to meet the people with officials and the police after the elections.

Is it not the responsibility of the people to contain the atrocities of the elected representatives of the people? Now we know how soon our elected representatives forget the problems of the people. Our leaders are enacting a drama before the people during the elections. The elected representatives feel happy when they are respected by the elites of the society. But they do not respect the ordinary people. They indulge in atrocities with impunity. They find time to attend functions and programmes but they do not find time to meet the people and listen to them. The representative democracy should not be allowed to stagnate and stink. It must be made into a vibrant reality.

It is a wrong belief that democracy starts and ends in elections. It goes beyond the elections. It can be nurtured in society as a culture. Democracy is a culture. People should have faith in it. In the beliefs and the actions of the people democracy should be reflected. It is a process by which decisions have to be taken, committees and councils have to be conducted. Respecting each other, valuing the views of each other, resolving problems on a consensus basis will determine the quality of democracy. We should not impose our ideas on the people. It is against the human will. Once Abraham Lincoln said, "I will not be a master and neither will I be a slave". The representative democracy expects that people should feel that the others are also having skills and knowledge. They can also decide. Democracy will not survive on the master-servant relationship.

I have an idea. I propose this to you for consideration. Whether you accept or reject it, it is up to you. It should be the attitude of the people in a democracy. It is a process by which a democratic society will be created. For the success of this representative democracy, the democratic culture has to be nurtured in the society. Society has to be democratized. It should be practised in the social institutions. Unless the society is prepared, oriented and transformed in consonance with the democratic culture, the representative democracy cannot deliver the goods and the services. Our society is based on equality as everyone gets only one vote. But in the society you find all kinds of discriminations and differences. We should not be unpleasant with what we have achieved. To get meaningful political equality, social equality is essential. Today we do not have such a kind of society. When we question the monarchy, why are we not questioning the discriminations. When we face problems in the elections, they are to be solved and the system has to be perfected. The role of money in the electoral process has to be eliminated. By doing all these things we can protect our representative democracy.

APPENDIX V

About the Author

It is a curious question to many about my political identity and social identity. Some believe that I am a person with Congress leanings and for a few I am a Left oriented person. For many my identity is towards the Dravidian movement. I move with all political parties and leaders for some specific people oriented activities. I have never sought any political help from any leader for my career or for my family. I enjoy the goodwill and affection of all political leaders. Those who interacted with me closely on public matters continuously will identify me very easily. Others are always guessing since I have worked with many political parties and leaders on many issues. Many of my friends who had political ambitions moved close to a party, joined the party and enhanced their position through the party. But I did not have such an ambition. I have to work for the people from a different platform. I enjoy this work. By keeping us away from politics but moving close to party leaders on issues affecting the people we can get the needed support from the leaders. We can keep our identity and protect our self respect. Hence I chose teaching, research and outreach activities. I love teaching and research. I like outreach programmes. Till date I enjoy teaching, research and conducting outreach programmes. A teacher can do effectively many works socially useful outside the institution provided he/she has commitment. From the academic platform many public activities can be carried out by which one can help governance, administration, civil society and so on. At present, I am involved in strengthening Panchayati Raj Institutions through training, policy advocacy and media sensitization.

From my childhood I evinced keen interest in politics as one of my close relatives was an MLC and he was close to K. Kamaraj. When I was a small boy I met many Congress leaders in my native town. I can recollect my first interaction with P. Nedumaran in my native village. In a small village my family struggled even for survival. As I grew, I came to realize that the existing social structure became an impediment and I felt that the Indian National Congress did not address the issues of the social structure. At that point of time, I was fascinated that the Dravidian movement started addressing the issues, which drew my attention. Till I completed my schooling I did not have any strong political likes and dislikes. I was fascinated by the freedom struggle and the dedicated service of the Congressmen. Every year activities were carried out in the schools to celebrate Independence Day and Republic Day and on all the occasions we were involved. As a result we were oriented to understand and appreciate the freedom struggle. But, on seeing the socio-economic conditions, I was not convinced of the programmes and policies of the Indian National Congress and I hated the feudalistic outlook of the Congress which drove me towards the Dravidian movement. All through I was active in public affairs. Even when I was in school I was very active in all extracurricular activities. When I was a researcher in Annamalai University, I was in prison for a month for the cause of the teachers.

After I became deeply involved in research, I changed my perspective and preferences. I remain in the public domain and I take a position based on issues. My perspective is Gandhian: Take a position to help the poor, the affected, the marginalized and the voiceless was the position of Gandhi. As long I was in Annamalai University as a student, as a researcher and as a teacher, I moved closely with the Leftists and the supporters of the Dravidian movement. On many of the occasions, I prefered to be with the Left as the Dravidian parties started moving away from the core values.

Ever since I moved over to Gandhigram Rural University, I got oriented in the Gandhian framework of activities. Hence I started moving towards the society more closely in a systematic way through our outreach programmes. Being the leader of a department I have conceptualized our academic, research and outreach programmes. Acadmic programmes should be relevant to the social needs, research should be socially relevant and outreach programme should make an impact. In this context, I have designed a five-year integrated M.A. programme in Development Administration to create a cadre of Development Managers and I have designed yet another M.A. programme in Governance and Development (two years) to cater to the needs of bilateral and multilateral development agencies. All our research activities are oriented towards grassroots governance, democracy, administration and development.

Our outreach programmes are designed with a view to enhancing the leadership and managerial skills of the grassroots elected representatives and inject professionalism into the activities of the functionaries at the grassroots. Thus Panchayati Raj activities are the major activities of our department. We established the Rajiv Gandhi Chair for Panchayati Raj Studies. It was Gandhigram Rural Institute which proposed the creation of the Rajiv Gandhi Chair. It was supported by the Rajiv Gandhi Foundation under the leadership of Ms. Sonia Gandhi. All our activities are supported by various agencies like the Ford Foundation, DANIDA, Population Foundation of India, UNDP, State Planning Commission, Ministry of Rural Development, Ministry of Panchayati Raj, World Bank, SDC, The Hunger Project, Institute of Social Sciences and PRIA.

I was drawn towards political parties to offer training to their MLAs and Local Body leaders. All my contact with party leaders are on Local Governance. Though I concentrate much on local governance, whenever my services are needed, the political parties have used my services because I used to write articles and books on politics, governance, administration, democracy and development periodically which made me familiar with many of the political parties and leaders. Though I am in a university teaching students, doing research and carrying out extension programmes, I continue to work with political parties with a view to injecting professionalism and commitment on the vital issues of governance, administration, development democracy, poverty eradication and prosperity achievement. Some of the leaders are close to me and seek my opinion, views and observations on certain key issues. All our works are periodically brought to popular consumption as we work on socially relevant issues.

Index